MIND SCULPTING REALITY

How To Sculpt Your Life Into Reality, One Story At A Time.

GERARD GROGANS

Copyright © 2025 by Gerard Grogans All rights reserved.

This book may not be reproduced in whole or in part, stored in a retrieval system, or transmitted in any form or by any means — electronic, mechanical, or other — without written permission from the publisher, except by a reviewer, who may quote brief passages in a review. The material in this book is intended for education. No expressed or implied guarantee of the effects of the use of the recommendations can be given nor liability taken.

FOREWORD

By Corey Poirier, Founder of bLU Talks

When I first encountered the concept of *Mind Sculpting Reality*, I knew I was holding something special in my hands. It wasn't just another book on mindset or personal growth—this was something deeper, something that struck at the very core of how we create and experience our lives.

What sets *Mind Sculpting Reality* apart is its ability to blend profound wisdom with practical tools, wrapped in a storytelling style that speaks directly to the soul. The author doesn't just tell us that transformation is possible; they walk us through it, step by step, sharing relatable stories, thought-provoking analogies, and actionable strategies that help us take back control of our lives.

In the work I do with bLU Talks, I've had the privilege of connecting with world-class leaders, speakers, and thinkers. The most impactful voices are always those who have lived through their own transformations and turned their experiences into blueprints for others to follow. This book is exactly that—a roadmap that empowers the reader to identify the stories they've been telling themselves and sculpt new ones that align with who they are at their core.

If you are someone who has ever felt stuck in your circumstances, overwhelmed by past experiences, or unsure how to move forward, *Mind Sculpting Reality* will serve as the guide you didn't know you needed.

It will challenge you, inspire you, and—most importantly—it will equip you to shape a reality you once thought was out of reach.

The world needs more people who live authentically and fully from the depths of who they are. This book is a powerful tool to help you become one of them.

I'm honored to share this foreword and invite you to embark on this life-changing journey.

With deep respect and gratitude,

Corey Poirier, Founder of bLU Talks

Award-Winning Speaker | Multiple-Time TEDx Speaker | Best-Selling Author | Podcast Host | Leadership and Personal Development Expert

WHAT OTHERS HAVE TO SAY

Gerard Grogans' "Mind Sculpting Reality" is a masterful guide to reshaping the way we think, feel, and perceive the world around us. His insights into the subconscious mind and practical exercises empower readers to break free from limiting beliefs and create the life they truly desire. This book is an essential resource for anyone on a journey of self-transformation." — Dr. Sofia Pierce, PhD in Cognitive Behavioral Therapy

"Grogans takes us on a fascinating journey into the depths of our own minds. By combining neuroscience with real-world application, he shows how anyone can consciously sculpt their reality by understanding and harnessing the power of their thoughts. A must-read for anyone interested in personal development and cognitive mastery." — Professor William Grant, Expert in Neuroscience and Consciousness Studies

"This book offers a practical and empowering blueprint for changing your life by changing your mind. Grogans masterfully explains how our thoughts shape our reality and offers actionable steps to break free from mental constraints. A groundbreaking and essential tool for those who seek lasting personal transformation." — Dr. Rachel Simmons, Clinical Psychologist and Author of Rewire Your Mind for Success

"Gerard Grogans' "Mind Sculpting Reality" is a brilliant work that seamlessly blends science and self-help. His approach to using mindfulness, meditation, and cognitive restructuring as tools for transforming your life is both profound and practical. It's a perfect read for anyone ready to make real and lasting changes." — Dr. Jason Williams, Therapist and Mindfulness Coach

"Grogans offers a groundbreaking approach to personal transformation. By understanding how the mind works and leveraging that knowledge, "Mind Sculpting Reality" shows us that the power to change our circumstances lies within. This is an indispensable resource for those committed to creating a fulfilling life." — Professor Linda Turner, Author of The Psychology of Personal Empowerment

"In "Mind Sculpting Reality", Grogans provides readers with scientifically backed techniques to reshape not just their minds but their entire lives. His insightful analysis of neuroplasticity and the subconscious mind empowers readers to become the architects of their own reality. I highly recommend this book to anyone serious about unlocking their potential." — Dr. Henry Adams, Neurologist and Author of Brain Hacks for Success

"This book is a game-changer! Grogans has created a roadmap for how to use our mental and emotional resources to design the life we've always dreamed of. "Mind Sculpting Reality" is a must-read for anyone who wants to move beyond self-doubt and step into their highest potential." — Dr. Olivia Hart, Transformational Life Coach

"Grogans' work is an eye-opener. His combination of psychological principles, practical techniques, and real-life examples provides readers with a powerful toolkit to change their thought patterns and reshape their lives. This is not just another self-help book—it's a manual for mastering your mind." — Professor Michael Roberts, Expert in Behavioral Economics

"Grogans offers profound insight into the power of mindset and thought. His approach combines scientific understanding with actionable steps, guiding readers to break through mental blocks and build a new reality from the inside out. It's a transformative and practical guide to creating lasting change." — Dr. Evelyn Moore, Positive Psychology Specialist

"In "Mind Sculpting Reality", Gerard Grogans invites readers to rethink their perceptions of reality and their own abilities. His techniques for mind mastery are practical and accessible, making this book an invaluable resource for anyone looking to take control of their destiny and sculpt a life of success, peace, and fulfillment." — Dr. Nathan Brooks, Expert in Personal Development and Author of The Psychology of Self-Mastery

TABLE OF CONTENTS

Foreword 3

What Others Have To Say 5

Introduction 1

Preview 3

About The Author 7

Chapter 1: Storytelling And Story Analysis 8

Chapter 2: Crafting Your Vision 38

Chapter 3: Reverse Engineering Your Vision 69

Chapter 4: Turn Your Vision Into A To-Do-List 78

Chapter 5: Programming Your Brain And Subconscious Mind 86

Chapter 6: How To Hypnotize Yourself For Greatness 112

Chapter 7: Restate Your Intentions 121

Chapter 8: How To Manifest Wealth And Success 139

Chapter 9: How To Sell Yourself To Others 145

Chapter 10: Build And Develop A Team 154

Chapter 11: Create Your Market Strategy 164

Chapter 12: Get Mad (Massive Action Daily) 185

Chapter Summaries 190

INTRODUCTION

Imagine standing before a raw block of stone, knowing that within it lies a masterpiece waiting to be uncovered. With each careful strike of your chisel, a vision of something remarkable begins to take shape, something that was beneath the surface hidden all along. This is what transformation feels like: the process of revealing the greatness already inside you.

Now picture being able to peel away the layers of doubt and fear, exposing the hidden potential beneath. What if the person you were always meant to be was already inside of you, waiting to be revealed? What if everything you've searched for was waiting for you to unlock it? That's exactly what *"Mind Sculpting Reality"* will help you do. It will help you bring out the best version of yourself and uncover the answers you've been seeking.

"Mind Sculpting Reality" isn't just another self-help book. It's the chisel you've been searching for; the tool to help you reshape your life into the masterpiece it was always meant to be. It's not about empty motivation or quick fixes; it's about helping you unlock the power within you that is always inside of you, using the lessons that come from your past to build the future you deserve.

Why? Because so many of us are held captive by our past, fixated on what went wrong instead of seeing the wisdom it offers. But what if you could change that? What if every setback, every victory, every moment—good or bad—was a steppingstone to the person you're meant to become?

It's time to stop letting life happen to you and it's time to start crafting the life you were always meant to live. *"Mind Sculpting Reality"* isn't about offering empty promises, it's about giving you the tools you need to reframe your past, extract its lessons, and align your actions with your deepest purpose and desires.

It's a blueprint for lasting transformation—a guide to rewriting the invisible scripts that run your life. It's not about quick fixes or fleeting motivation. It's about rewiring the way you think, breaking free from the habits that hold you back, and creating a mindset that propels you toward the life you've always envisioned.

The fact that you're holding this book means you're ready to start. The tools you need are right here, and the masterpiece of your life is waiting to be revealed. So, if you're ready.

Let's start sculpting it.

PREVIEW

Chapter 1: Storytelling and Story Analysis

In this chapter, we will explore the power of storytelling and how to analyze your life experiences. You will sift through your past, uncover the recurring themes and patterns that define your journey, and discover the common thread that connects all your life stories. This will help you develop your "Identity Statement"—a foundational tool that tells you who you are, who you're meant to serve, and how you're meant to serve them. Understanding this core identity is crucial for everything that comes next.

Chapter 2: Crafting Your Vision

Your vision is your compass. Without it, you're drifting aimlessly. In this chapter, you'll learn how to create a vision for your life that is clear, compelling, and achievable. We'll break down the RAPS framework—Realistic, Achievable, Predictable and Sustainable—to ensure that your goals are within reach. A well-defined vision will keep you motivated, even when obstacles arise. Learn how to dream big but stay grounded in reality as you build a future worth striving for.

Chapter 3: Reverse Engineering Your Vision

Here, you will take your big vision and break it down into smaller, actionable steps. This chapter builds on Stephen Covey's idea of "beginning with the end in mind."

You'll learn how to reverse-engineer your life goals, starting with the end result and working backward to figure out the exact steps needed to get there. Whether it's writing a book, launching a business, or building a personal brand, reverse-engineering your goals will make achieving them a clear and manageable process.

Chapter 4: Turn Your Vision into a To-Do-List

Now that you've broken your vision into smaller steps, it's time to get to work. This chapter focuses on turning your goals into a daily to-do list. We'll discuss the power of list-making and how it helps condition your brain to focus on one task at a time. A well-organized to-do list will keep you on track and help you make steady progress toward your goals every day.

Chapter 5: Program Your Brain and Subconscious Mind

In this chapter, you'll learn how to program your mind for success. Our thoughts shape our reality, and by reprogramming your subconscious, you can eliminate limiting beliefs and negative self-talk. We'll explore techniques like visualization, affirmations, and neuro-linguistic programming (NLP) to help you cultivate a mindset that supports your goals and fuels your growth.

Chapter 6: How to Hypnotize Yourself for Greatness

Self-hypnosis is a powerful tool for reprogramming your subconscious mind and breaking through mental barriers. In this chapter, you'll discover how to use self-hypnosis techniques to unlock hidden potential and create a mindset that attracts success. By tapping into your subconscious, you can overcome fears, build confidence, and manifest your desires more effectively.

Chapter 7: Restate Your Intentions

In this chapter, you'll learn the importance of restating your intentions regularly. Consistent affirmation of your goals and identity helps solidify them in your subconscious mind. By consciously affirming your purpose and direction, you create a mental environment that promotes success and eliminates self-doubt.

Chapter 8: How to Manifest Wealth and Success

Wealth and success don't just happen—they're the result of intentional actions and aligned thinking. This chapter will teach you how to manifest financial abundance and success by applying the principles of attraction and belief. Learn how to shift your mindset around money and success and watch as your reality begins to align with your desires.

Chapter 9: How to Sell Yourself to Others

In order to succeed, you must first sell yourself. Whether you're building a business, seeking a promotion, or simply influencing others, this chapter will teach you the art of self-promotion and persuasion. You'll learn how to craft your personal story, present yourself confidently, and communicate your value in a way that others can't resist.

Chapter 10: Build and Develop a Team

No one achieves success alone. In this chapter, you'll learn how to build a team that shares your vision and helps you achieve your goals. We'll explore the keys to leadership, how to recruit the right people, and how to foster a collaborative environment that accelerates your success.

Chapter 11: Create Your Marketing Strategy

Every business or idea needs visibility. In this chapter, we'll dive into marketing strategy, teaching you how to effectively market yourself, your products, and your ideas. Whether through digital channels, word of mouth, or traditional methods, you'll learn how to create a marketing plan that amplifies your voice and brings your message to the world.

Chapter 12: Get MAD

In the final chapter, we'll talk about the power of Motivation, Action, and Discipline (MAD). Success isn't about knowing what to do, it's about doing it.

You'll learn how to stay motivated, take consistent action, and develop the discipline to keep moving forward, no matter what obstacles arise.

This chapter will inspire you to push through the hard times and stay committed to your goals. Each chapter of *"Mind Sculpting Reality"* offers a unique insight into how you can transform your life from the inside out.

As you journey through these pages, you'll uncover your core identity, craft a vision for your future, and begin taking actionable steps toward creating the life you've always dreamed of. The power is within you, and this book will show you how to unlock it.

So, let's get started!

ABOUT THE AUTHOR

Gerard Grogans is a world-renowned transformational author, speaker, coach, and trainer, who is celebrated for his ability to help individuals break through mental and emotional barriers and unlock their full potential. With a rare combination of expertise in personal development, human behavior, and psychology, Gerard excels in guiding his clients to profound, lasting change. His work goes beyond traditional coaching by addressing the root causes of limitations—transforming mindsets, healing emotional wounds, and empowering individuals to become the highest versions of themselves.

What truly distinguishes Gerard as a transformational coach is his deep understanding of both the psychological and metaphysical aspects of human development. With a BA in Sacred Theology, a BA in Psychology, and a Doctorate in Metaphysical Psychology, Gerard has spent years studying the mind-body-spirit connection. His unique academic background enables him to address the holistic nature of transformation, combining the science of psychology with the deeper, spiritual dimensions of personal growth and development. However, it wasn't always that way. Like many of the individuals he coaches, Gerard has faced his own mental barriers, self-doubt, and limiting beliefs. He has walked the path of transformation, learning to master his own psychology, overcome obstacles, and step into his purpose. Through years of rigorous self-development, Gerard not only healed his own wounds but also discovered the tools and strategies that allowed him to help others break free from their own limiting beliefs.

For more information on how to work with Gerard go to: www.gerardgrogans.com

STORYTELLING AND STORY ANALYSIS

"Life isn't about finding yourself. Life is about creating yourself."

– George Bernard Shaw

George Bernard Shaw's timeless words serve as a powerful reminder that we don't discover our true selves through a sudden moment of revelation. Instead, we shape who we are through the choices we make and the decisions we commit to. This idea is at the core of every self-help and personal development book you've ever read.

Why? Because the simple truth is that you don't simply stumble upon your authentic self; you must intentionally create it. Therefore, to become the person you're truly meant to be, you must first understand who you've been in the past.

Why? Because every decision you've made, every challenge you've faced, and yes, even every mistake you've learned from, has contributed to shaping the person you are today. Whether those experiences were positive or negative, they have all played a role in your evolution.

Thus, the age-old adage still holds true: "We become what we think about the most." Why? Because your past holds the key to your future. By examining your past, you'll not only uncover the patterns and behaviors that have subtly shaped your thoughts and actions, but you'll also gain clarity about who you're consciously meant to become.

Why? Because your past isn't just a record; it's the blueprint for who you're destined to be.

Defining Moments in your Life

Okay so, let's pause for a moment and reflect on the three defining moments of your life. Why? Because these moments have been pivotal in shaping the person you are today. But here's the important part: this exercise isn't just about reminiscing—it's about uncovering the patterns and behaviors woven into these stories, so you can turn them into powerful insights.

And so, here's what I'd like you to do: grab a blank sheet of paper and write out each defining moment in your life, as a full story. Why? Because when you write them down as stories, they become real. Seeing these moments on paper makes it easier for you to spot the subtle patterns and behaviors that continue to influence you, often below the surface, without your awareness.

And so, the more you understand how your past has shaped your present, the clearer the path to your future will become. Why? Because these stories hold the lessons you've learned—and it's through these lessons that you'll find a framework for how you can teach what you've learned to uplift and inspire others to change as well.

Your task is simply to identify the three defining moments that have had the greatest impact on you, the lessons learned, and how you can use those lessons to help someone else, who may be going through what you've been through. It's about recognizing the recurring patterns and behaviors that have left their mark on you.

Now, let's dive into these questions to guide your reflection:

- What are the experiences that have brought you the most pain or the most pleasure in your life?

- What are the experiences that have shaped who you are today and still linger in your thoughts?

- What are the biggest mistakes you've made, and what did you learn from them?

- Who has had the greatest impact on your life, and what lessons have you drawn from them, whether positive or negative?

- If you had no doubts, fears, or limiting beliefs holding you back, what would you do today?

- Do you feel your life is heading in the right direction or do you feel stuck, unsure of what you're meant to do?

- What if I told you that you could create the reality you desire right now. But the first step you needed to take was to learn how to turn your stories of trauma into a teachable framework that could help someone else?

- What would you say is the biggest obstacle standing in your way?

Answering all these questions will not only help you recognize the recurring patterns and behaviors that have been holding you back, and keeping you from reaching your full potential. But they will also reveal to you the steps you need to take in order to break free from the recurring patterns and behaviors running in the background of your unconscious awareness.

Why? Because as I've already stated, we are all the totality of all our life experiences and it is those life experiences that not only teach us who we are but also who we're meant to be in the future once we learn how to use them to our advantage.

Discovery Process

Now that you've reflected on your defining moments, it's time to dive deeper. Look for the keywords, phrases, or patterns that keep emerging across your stories.

Why? Because by identifying these recurring elements, you can begin to understand *why* you do the things you do and *why* you think the way you think.

And so, from these patterns, we can uncover the lessons you've learned and find the common thread that runs through your life. This is where we begin to identify what I call your "Identity Statement."

Why is this important? Because your "Identity Statement" is the driving force behind everything you think, say, and do. It's what makes you come alive because it reflects your true, authentic self, the person you're meant to be, deep down inside. This statement is reflected in the books you read, the people you surround yourself with, the environment you grew up in, and even the way you were raised.

When you uncover your "Identity Statement," everything else in your life will begin to align. Why? Because it holds the key to your future. It's the guiding force that directs your path, and the only way to find it is by examining the common themes running through your life and pinpointing what your "Identity Statement" means to you. Once you discover it, you'll have the clarity to live in alignment with your true purpose.

What is your common theme?

Okay so, to truly understand this, let's break it down even further. Why? Because every story in your life has a common theme—a central moment that lies at the heart of all your internal struggles. These struggles are the very ones you're grappling with right now, the ones keeping you up at night, the ones you wish someone could help you solve. Am I right?

And so, here's the thing: those same struggles will lead you to understand the people you're meant to serve because they're dealing with the same issues. They, too, are struggling with the same challenges that you've faced—and overcome.

Why does this matter? Because each of us possesses a unique set of talents and skills that make us better equipped to do things better or differently than anyone else. These unique abilities aren't just for us; they're meant to help the people we're destined to serve.

The very same people who are lying awake at night, hoping to find someone who can help them solve the same problems we've already overcome.

This is why your "Identity Statement" is so crucial. Why? Because understanding your "Identity Statement" doesn't just bring clarity to *who* you are—it illuminates *who* you're meant to serve and *how* you can serve them. They're looking for someone who truly understands their struggle, someone who can guide them through the exact challenges you've already faced by showing them a clear roadmap or step-by-step framework. And that's where you and I come in.

Discovered Your "Identity Statement."

And so, if it's alright with you, I'd love to share how I came to identify my own "Identity Statement." To do this, I'll take you through three defining moments that have shaped me into the person I am today. My hope is that by hearing these stories, you'll see how they led me to discover my own "Identity Statement"—and how the process might help you understand yours.

Okay so, let me take you back to June 1985. My brother Jason and I had just got off the school bus, heading home, with a mix of excitement, nervousness, and fear because it was report card day.

Like most boys, we were joking and playing around, running and tagging each other as we walked. Suddenly, my brother turned to me with a mischievous grin on his face and said, "Hey, Bigshot" (a nickname my grandmother had given me because she always said I'd be a bigshot one day).

He smiled and said, "If you show me your report card, I'll show you mine."

Back then, report cards were a bit different. Teachers could use red ink to highlight your struggles, making sure your parents knew exactly how poorly you were doing in school.

I remember telling Jason, "Alright, but same time, same time." He agreed, "Okay, show me yours, and I'll show you mine."

When Jason handed me his report card, my heart sank. It was covered in D's and F's, with a whole lot of red ink.

The first thought that rushed into my mind was, *Man, you're in trouble. They're really going to get you.*

To be fair, my grades weren't perfect either. They weren't all A's and B's. But at least I had a few C's and D's sprinkled in there—not just an endless string of D's and F's like Jason's.

When we got home, Mom was already waiting at the door, her expression a mix of anticipation and maternal dread. She greeted us with, "Boys, let me see those report cards. I know it's report card day, so don't even think about trying to hide them.

I hesitated, reluctant to show her mine. It wasn't great, but it wasn't as bad as Jason's—at least I had that going for me. With a reluctant sigh, I reached into my bag and handed over my report card. She studied it for a moment before looking at me with those piercing mom's eyes. "Gerard," she said, "you can do better than this, can't you?"

"Yes, ma'am," I muttered. Meanwhile, Jason saw his opening and bolted for the kitchen, trying to dodge the inevitable.

"Jason!" Mom called out. "Bring me your report card. I know you got yours, too."

"They didn't give it to me," Jason tried to bluff.

Mom wasn't having it. "Boy, stop lying. I know you have it, so you might as well hand it over."

With a sheepish shuffle, Jason handed her his report card. Mom took one look and shook her head, disbelief written all over her face. "I don't know what you boys are doing in school," she said, her voice heavy with disappointment. "But when your dad gets home, he's going to have a word with both of you."

She waved us off toward the kitchen. "Go get something to eat and wait for your father to come home."

A few minutes later, Dad walked through the door, and we could tell from the slam of the screen door that he wasn't in a good mood. Mom didn't waste any time, she handed him our report cards without a word.

The next thing we knew, he stormed into the kitchen where Jason and I were quietly eating.

"Look at these report cards!" he yelled. "What in the hell are you kids doing in school? You're obviously not there to learn!" He waved the papers like they were evidence in a trial, his voice rising with every syllable. "Dumb, Stupid, Lazy ass kids…you'll never amount to anything!"

Each word hit me like a slap. I sat there, as the anger bubbled up inside me. In my head, I shouted back at him, *No, YOU'RE the stupid one. YOU'RE the one who doesn't know anything. Just wait. I'll show you.*

At that moment, I made a conscious decision—a vow, really. I would prove him wrong. I would be better. I would do better. His words might have been meant to tear me down, but they became fuel for my fire.

And then I heard Mom's voice echo in my mind: "You can do better than this." It wasn't just a reprimand; it was a challenge. A belief. A reminder that I had the power to rise above.

That moment—sitting at the kitchen table, swallowing my anger and shame—became a defining point in my life.

As I've looked back on all the key moments that have shaped who I am, there's a common thread: a determination to *be better* and *do better*. It's the force that drives every decision I make, every step I take. And it all started with a report card and a father's scorn that I refused to let define me.

Finding Your One Word

This powerful realization led me to uncover a single word that has become the bedrock of everything I think, feel, and do. This word is the foundation of my personal "Identity Statement"—and it can be yours too. Why is this so crucial? Because when you take the time to reflect on the three defining moments of your life, you'll discover a thread, a common theme, and ultimately, a word that speaks directly to the heart of who you are.

Your task is to identify that word and turn it into a statement—an affirmation that encapsulates your true essence and becomes the guiding principle for every step you take moving forward.

Here's why: at some point in your life, you made a decision that has set you on the course you're on today. This decision may have shaped your path in ways that either uplifted you or held you back.

In either case, it has likely shaped the person you are now. You may have reached a level of success—on paper, everything looks good—but inside it still feels like something is missing. There's a sense of incompleteness, an unfulfilled potential lingering beneath the surface.

That's why it's time to pause and reflect on the experiences that have molded and shaped you. Why? Because your one word and the common theme that runs through your life is what defines who you are at the core and who you're meant to serve. Your job is to distill it into an "Identity

Statement" that not only defines who you are but also clarifies what you do, at your deepest level.

Finding this one word is transformative. It's the key to recognizing what truly sets you apart from everyone else. It's your personal blueprint that embodies the essence of who you are. When you uncover it, it becomes the foundation for everything that follows, guiding you toward the life you were always meant to live.

Draft Your Identity Statement

Okay so, now it's your time to draft "Your Identity Statement." Why? Because your "Identity Statement" not only determines who you are and what you do, but it also identifies who you're meant to serve and how you're meant to serve them because it aligns with who you are at the core, your true authentic self. And so, I don't want you to get discouraged when coming up with your "Identity Statement."

Just keep in mind that it is the first draft and will more than likely change over time as you continue to refine it and make it your own as you begin to understand what it is that you actually do and how you do it. But for now, just write something out and keep working on it as you go along the way.

But remember to:

- Keep it simple and clear.

- Make it actionable and measurable.

- Make sure it is a reflection of who you are at the core and make sure it describes what you do, who you serve, and how you serve them that truly resonates with you.

Okay so, your "Identity Statement" should be formatted like this, or something close to it:

I HELP_____ DO THIS _____

SO THAT THEY_____CAN DO_____

Once you've identified your "Identity Statement", the next thing you need to do is to identify what I call your "I Am Statement."

Determine Your "I Am Statement"

Why? Because your "I Am Statement" also embodies who you truly are at the core, but it also tells the world what you have declared yourself to be. And so, I want you to think about it like this. If you could do or be anyone in the world that you wanted to be based on who you've been in the past, and the lessons you've learned from all your life experiences.

- Who would you be?

- And what would you call yourself?

Why? Because if you don't know who you truly want to be or what you would call yourself, it will be almost impossible to become that person because you don't believe that that's who you truly are at your core. And so, the reason why we've been focusing on helping you identify your "Identity Statement", is because that's who you are at the core.

And so, let me see if I can give you another example of what I mean from my own "Identity Statement. Okay so, remember the story of my brother Jason and I coming home with our report cards and our mother meeting us at the door, and after seeing my report card she said, Gerard, you can do better than this.

Well in that same story after my dad was yelling, and screaming at us, I decided to make a conscious decision to prove him wrong. Those two experiences led me to understand that the core of what I do is to be better and do better and that everything I do is about transforming myself to be the best version of myself that I can be.

And so, my one word is transformation and the reason why I call myself the #1 transformational speaker trainer in the world is for two reasons.

1. One I decided that's who I wanted to be based on the common theme and one word that runs through my life.

2. And two, I've done everything within my power to become that person. And you must do it too!

Why? Because your "One Word" and your "Identity Statement" are a declaration to the world that this is who you are, and this is who you have declared yourself to be.

Why? Because to reiterate what George Bernard Shaw said, "Life isn't about finding yourself. Life is about creating yourself." Am I Right? And so, you must do everything within your power to become that person that you know you're meant to be deep down inside, no matter how long it takes.

This includes reading, studying, and learning everything you need to learn in order to become the person you have declared yourself to be. And so, my "I Am Statement" is that I am the # 1 Transformational Speaker Trainer in the world because everything I do is about helping people transform themselves into the best version of themselves that they can be. This comes from me knowing what my "One Word" is (transformation), and the common theme that runs through my own life which is "Be Better, Do Better." And now it's your turn to do the same!

Why? Because before you can become the person you know you're truly destined to be, you must identify what your "One Word" is. And so, below I've included a list of words that you can use to help you identify what your "One Word" is or could be based on the word that resonates with you the most; the "One Word" that you believe defines who you are at the core.

But again, keep in mind that these are just suggestions and that your "One Word" may be different. So don't feel restricted or think that you have to use any of these words, they are just suggestions that other people have used as their "One Word." Just look at the list as a form of inspiration to see if any of these words resonate with you the most:

#Action	#Focus	#Present
#Adapt	#Fortitude	#Purpose
#Adventure	#Freedom	#Rebuilding
#Ambition	#Grace	#Reduce
#Balance	#Growth	#Reflection
#Battle	#Ignite	#Relentless
#Be	#Imagine	#Resolve
#Brave	#Invest	#Revel
#Celebrate	#Learn	#Risk
#Change	#Listen	#Shine
#Commit	#Love	#Silence
#Confidence	#Mindfulness	#Simplify
#Courage	#Minimize	#Soar
#Curious	#Momentum	#Strength
#Dare	#Open	#Thrive
#Determined	#Opportunity	#Together
#Direction	#Optimism	#Transformation
#Discover	#Organize	#Transition
#Empathy	#Peace	#Unstoppable
#Empower	#Persistence	#Uplift
#Finish	#Possibility	

Okay so, after you've found your "One Word", now it's time to take it to the next level. And so, here's what I want you to do.

I want you to take your "One Word" and I want you to make a declaration to yourself and the world that says, this is who you are and what you stand for as the person you have declared yourself to be. Why? Because this will become your personal manifesto and mission statement for everything you think and do. Because it will be intrinsically connected to your "One Word" and the common theme that runs through your life.

Use "Your Identity Statement" to Define What You Actually Do"

Okay so, now that you've discovered your "Identity Statement," the next step is to use it as a tool to clarify *what* it is that you actually do. Why? Because your "Identity Statement" and your "I Am Statement" are the keys that unlock your "How to Statement."

This is where things get practical. Why? Because your "How to Statement" is the roadmap that takes someone from where they are right now—Point A—to where they want to be—Point B. It's the clear, step-by-step process that you'll guide them towards getting the transformation they want. It is based on the same journey you went on to go from Point A to Point B in your own life and the methods you use to help someone else get those same results.

This is where your purpose and your expertise merge to create real, tangible results for others. Am I right? And don't worry if you don't get all of the steps exactly right at this point, because they will probably change as you start to become the leading expert in your field.

Why? Because the more you can learn to organize and curate the data and information that you know or that you've learned though self-study and by mastering yourself, the easier it will be for you to put that data and information into a teachable framework that you can then begin to teach to someone else. Am I Right?

This is the essence of what you offer to the world: a proven, actionable path that others can follow with you because it's grounded in who you are at the core. Later, I'll show you how to take this same outline and expound upon it so that everything you know and teach begins to fit together into a chronological step-by-step order that you then begin to teach to someone else.

Why? Because each one of us has a unique talent and skill that allows us to understand and absorb certain knowledge and information better than or differently than anyone else.

And so, it is our capacity to absorb this data and information that also reveals to us who we are and who we're meant to serve because again, it's based on who we are at the core.

Discovering Your Life's Purpose

And so, your capacity to read, study, and learn is an indicator of who you are, who you're meant to serve, and how you're meant to serve them. Am I Right? I mean, when you really think about it.

Each of us has a brain that is wired to learn and remember new data and new information that only we are equipped to study and learn. Each of us has a brain that's naturally geared towards becoming the leading expert in whatever chosen field we choose.

The problem is that many of us are not focused on who we are at the core and what we are called to do with our lives because we are so focused on being what others want us to be, instead of creating the life we want.

Each of us are born with an innate drive to master or be good at something but we never take the time to discover what that is based on who we are at the core. And so, here's the kicker! We learn the way we teach, and we teach the way we learn.

And so, what that means to you and me is that the more we can understand how our brain is naturally wired to read, study, and learn new data and information, the sooner we'll be able to identify what our true calling in life really is.

Okay so, for example, let's say that you've always had a gift of gab and a knack for storytelling as a kid, and you just love telling tales and captivating your friends with your imagination. And so, you spend all of your time and energy reading, studying, and learning how to tell great stories and present those stories in a way that captivates, engages, and holds your audience's attention.

You may find yourself drawn to a career in public speaking because you love entertaining people with your words and imagination.

Or let's say that you want to become a writer, filmmaker, or even a game designer because you love to write scripts or create video games. Do you think this would be a coincidence? No, it's because your brain is naturally wired to be a writer or video creator.

And so, your purpose in life is to find the thing that embodies who you are at the core and what you have a natural inclination to read, study, and learn because it is how you are uniquely wired.

Finding clarity

Okay so, once you have clarity on who you are, and what you have a natural ability to read, study and learn. It's time to take what you know and what you've learned and put it into a teachable framework that you can then begin to teach to others.

Why? Because it's one thing to know who you are and what it is that you do, but it's a totally different thing to take what you know and put it into a framework or step-by-step process that you can use to take someone from Point A to B, in the shortest and quickest time possible. Am I Right?

Brainstorm Ideas

Okay so, here's what I want you to do. I want you to grab a pen and a piece of paper or you can open up a new document on your computer. And I want you to start brainstorming ideas that come to mind based on what you believe it is that you do.

Don't overthink it, just allow whatever ideas come to mind naturally. And then you want to ask yourself:

- What are the things that come naturally to you that you're really good at? Or what are those things that you can do with your eyes closed that others may struggle with or have a problem with?

- What do people come to you for help with? Or what have you learned and studied through self-study or on-the-job training?

- What activities give you energy for days that you never get tired of?

- What can you do so well that you naturally do it without even thinking about it? What are those tasks or activities that you can do on autopilot, which are so ingrained in you that they've become second nature?

- What are the strengths, talents, and abilities that make you different and unique from everyone else? Or in other words, what are those qualities that set you apart from everyone else that make you, YOU?

- What knowledge, skills, and expertise have you mastered or acquired on your own, though either self-study or through your work/life experiences that gives you the confidence to believe that this is what you should be doing for the rest of your life?

- What are the lessons you've learned from everything that you've been reading, studying, or learning that you can put into a teachable framework that you can then begin to teach to someone else?

Identifying What You're Naturally Good At

Why? Because the more you can identify what you're naturally gifted at doing, the easier it will be to play to your strengths. Why? Because your "Sweet Spot" is that magical place where whatever you decide to do comes naturally to you because it comes from who you are at the core. It's usually something you love doing where you don't even have to think about it because it comes so naturally to you.

Identifying Your Sweet Spot

Okay so, here's what I want you to do. I want you to take out another sheet of paper and this time, I want you to draw three intersecting circles that overlap in the middle (see the following illustration below).

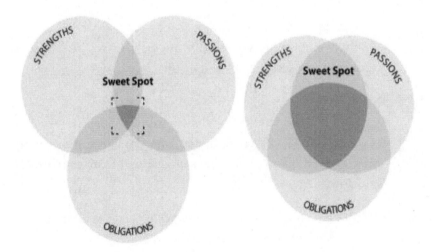

Step One:

In the first circle labeled 'Strengths', I want you to write all the things that come to mind that embody your strengths. Even those strengths that other people have told you about yourself that you may not have even realized.

Step Two:

In the second circle labeled 'Passion', I want you to write the words that you're passionate about. The things that you are most interested in — including all of the things that motivate and inspire you to make the changes you've made in your own life.

Why? Because the same things that you're motivated and passionate about are the same things that the people you're meant to serve are motivated and passionate about.

Step Three:

Moving on to the third circle labeled 'Obligations', I want you to add the word 'Commitments', to it as well.

Why? Because if you are not committed to becoming the leading expert in your field, then you'll give up with the going gets tough and you'll never reach your full potential. And do, in this space, I want you to jot down everything that you're committed to doing to become the person you have declared yourself to be, and to create the life that you want to create for yourself.

Why? Because without being totally committed to doing whatever you need to do to become the person you've declared yourself to be and creating the life you want to create, you won't stay the course and as I've said you'll give up when the going gets tough, and I don't want you to do that.

Finding Your Competitive Edge

That's why we need to find what your "Competitive Edge is. Why? Because it is your "Competitive Edge" that will give you a leg up on the people who are doing the same things you're doing and will help keep you focused on the end results.

Why? Because without knowing what your "Competitive Edge" and "Sweet Spot" is you'll just throw in the towel because you won't know what it is that sets you apart from everyone else, and you'll say to yourself, why should I do anything because somebody else is already doing what I want to do anyway.

Key Takeaway

And so, here's the thing: Yes, there will always be others doing what you want to do or creating what you want to create. But what sets you apart is simple—you're *you*, and they're not.

You were designed to be uniquely different from everyone else on the planet. Even if you're teaching the same material as someone else, no one can teach it the way you do. That's your superpower.

Think about it like this: Have you ever taken an algebra class where one teacher explains the material, and no matter how hard you try, it just doesn't click?

Then another teacher comes in and breaks it down in a completely different way, simple, relatable, in plain terms—and suddenly, the lightbulb goes on. It's not the content that changed; it's the teacher who made all the difference. Am I Right?

And so, in the same way, your unique voice, perspective, and approach are what set you apart. You bring something to the table that no one else can replicate, and that's exactly why people will resonate with you and the way you deliver your message.

Why? Because your "Competitive Edge" is the key to standing out in a crowded market. It's your unique perspective, your distinctive way of presenting and delivering familiar content—that makes you unlike anyone else. Think of it as the lens through which only *you* see the world, the special quality that differentiates you from everyone else doing similar work. It's the reason your voice resonates in a way theirs can't.

But here's the thing: uncovering your "Competitive Edge" and finding your "Sweet Spot" requires more than surface-level thinking. It demands a deeper dive, a genuine introspection into what truly makes you different. It's about understanding the unique combination of experiences, insights, and talents that shape how you approach your craft.

Therefore, the goal isn't just to know what sets you apart; it's to transform that uniqueness into a teachable framework. A method that is so clear and impactful that it empowers others to listen, learn, and apply your message to their own lives with ease. That's the essence of your "Competitive Edge"—it's not just what you do, but how only *you* can do it in a way that changes lives.

Do a Deeper Dive and Introspection into Who You Are!

Okay so, let's begin by taking a deeper dive into who you are at your core—exploring why you do the things you do and why you think the way you think. Why is this important?

Because while it might feel a bit repetitive, this process will bring you even closer to understanding what truly makes you different and unique.

Yes, we touched on this a little bit in the first chapter when we analyzed your stories to uncover the common theme running through your life. But now, we're going a little bit deeper. This isn't just about finding the thread; it's about unraveling *why* that thread exists in the first place.

It's about understanding the driving forces behind your actions, the beliefs that shape your decisions, and the motivations that fuel your journey.

Why? Because when you can learn to go beyond the surface of who you are and what you do, you'll truly understand the "why" behind your thoughts and actions, and you unlock an entirely new level of self-awareness. That's why everything we've been doing so far is to help you gain a greater sense of awareness about who you are and why you do the things you do. Because it will become the foundation for everything you'll create, teach, and share moving forward.

Okay so, let's dig in—because your uniqueness is not just what you do, but why you do it. Okay so, here's what I want you to do. I want you to back into your stories and I want you to ask yourself these qualifying questions to the three defining moments that have happened in your life. And I want you to analyze and psychoanalyze:

- Who's doing the talking?
- What's being said?
- How does it make you feel?
- What did they learn from it?

Why? Because the more you can relate to the emotional and psychological elements in your stories, the easier it will be for you to take the lessons you've learned and put them into a teachable framework that you can then begin to teach to someone else.

Why? Because the more you can understand the details of your own life stories and what you did to overcome them, the easier it will be for you to teach it to someone else because you understand the effects it has on you from a psychological and emotional level.

Teach what you know

Okay so, the first thing you want to do is break down what you already know (i.e., your knowledge, skills, expertise, and experiences), into a step-by-step framework or chronological order that you can then begin to teach to someone else.

Why? Because for one, it becomes that much easier for you to remember, and two it becomes that much easier for you to put it into a teachable framework that is easy for someone else to follow. Am I Right?

Why? Because the easier you can make something for someone else to understand, the easier it will be for them to apply what they're learning to the area of their lives where it is needed the most. So, the goal here is to break down what you already know into learning objectives that are easy to follow to help someone else overcome the problems, issues, and concerns they may be having, so they can get a specific and measurable result at the end of your training. Ain't That Right?

Why? Because the landmark of any great teacher is to be able to help someone else get the results they're looking for in the quickest and shortest time possible.

And so, your job as a coach, teacher, and trainer is to take the data and information that you've been curating and put it into a step-by-step framework that is easy to remember but that is also relevant to addressing your target audience's wants, needs, and desires. But it is also easy to follow and learn.

Why? Because when your target audience knows what actions, you want them to take, and they can see it clearly and concisely, they are more likely to take those actions because it's clear and easy to follow. And so, I want you to understand and get this picture clearly.

So, imagine that you are a master chef, and you've been cooking for over 10 years, and you've finally got this killer lasagna recipe that everyone wants to taste, because they say it's the best they've ever had, and they want you to teach them how to make it.

You don't just throw all the ingredients at them and say, "Go for it!" No, you break it down step-by-step and in chronological order so it's easy for them to follow. Am I Right?

You start with the basics, like how to choose the right tomatoes for the sauce, or the importance of using fresh basil. You explain why each step is crucial, like why you have to simmer the sauce for hours to get the flavors to meld together. You're not just teaching them how to follow a recipe; you're teaching them so that they truly understand and can do it all by themselves. Why? Because when people understand how to make your recipe using the strategies, principles, and techniques you've taught them. But you're giving them a skill they can use for the rest of their lives.

And so, the best part of this is when they serve your lasagna recipe to their friends and family, they too will have a smile on their faces, because they know how to put your recipe together properly, in the same way.

And so, whether you're a coach, teacher, or trainer, your job isn't just to transfer information.

It's to inspire, motivate, and train your target audience to equip them with the tools, strategies, and principles that can help them do what you do, even better. Why? Because that's the mark of a great teacher. Am I Right?

And so, that's why it is so important to keep asking the right questions because getting to the right answer takes focus and commitment before you can spark that flame of curiosity within yourself, much less anyone else.

And so, the first thing you need to do is become a student of yourself before you can become a teacher to someone else. Why? Because before you can properly teach and instruct someone else, you must first become an instrument of change in your own life. Am I Right?

The Purpose for Continuous Learning

And so, the first thing you must understand is leaders are readers. Why? Because reading, studying, and learning is a lifelong endeavor that never ends. So, you must maintain a consistent reading and studying program that will not only improve your content but also improve your teaching skills.

Secondly, you must learn to teach in a way that is accustomed to the way your target audience learns. That's why it is so important that you find out as much about them as you possibly can.

Why? Because let's say for example, you imagine that you're a fitness coach and you've been working out for years, and you've got the body to prove it. But if you can't communicate in a way that your target audience truly understands. Then it's like having a gold mine and not knowing how to dig.

You've got to be able to dig down into the trenches to truly understand what your target audience is struggling with and how you're going to help them overcome it. You've got to learn how to speak their language, and to connect with them on a deeper more personal level. Why? Because if you can't, then you're not really teaching. Am I Right?

And so, it's not just about helping them become their best selves, but it's about empowering them to want to make whatever life changes they want to make on their own.

Okay so, enough said because I've beaten this dead horse enough.

Now it's your turn!

Using Your Intuitive Mind to Reaffirm You're on The Right Track

Okay so, here's what I want you to do. I want you to use your intuitive mind to reaffirm that you're on the right track teaching what you know. Why? Because this is where all of your true knowledge and understanding comes from and your subconscious mind already knows what you should be doing with your life.

We just want to make sure that you're on track doing what you already know what you should be doing. Why? Because you don't want to spend all of your time and energy creating and working on something that is not in alignment with who you truly are and then realize later you should be doing something else. Am I Right?

Teach What You Know

And so, here's what I want you to do. I want you to close your eyes and picture yourself teaching what you already know to the people you're meant to be teaching it to. And I want you to visualize each step of your process to take someone from where they are Point A, to where they want to be Point B. Then I want you to ask yourself, if you were teaching what you know to someone else?

- How would you teach them?

- How can you break down what you know in a way that's easy for someone else to grasp and follow?

I know, I know that this may sound a little redundant, but I want to make sure that you understand what we're truly doing step-by-step. Why? Because your job is simply to bring focus and attention to what you already know and just allows your intuitive mind to teach you how to teach what you know to someone else.

What this will do is force your subconscious mind to bring to the forefront of your conscious mind all of the data and information that is most relevant to you and to your target audience. While also removing information that is not relevant to their journey.

Why? Because sometimes the information you're looking for will come instantly and other times it may come later as you let your mental focus and concentration go. Your job is just to trust that your subconscious mind will teach you because it already knows what you should be teaching in the first place. It is simply waiting for you to ask for the answers.

Either way, the goal of this exercise is simply just to allow your subconscious mind to use your brain's natural information-seeking mechanism to solve problems and get the solutions to the questions you're already asking. And so, when you learn to relax your mind and let go of what you think you should be teaching, your intuitive mind will naturally begin to seek and solve the questions you present to it.

Why? Because your brain has an innate ability to fill in gaps with anticipatory solutions based on what you already previously know and have experienced in your life.

So, what this will do is remove any information overload that you may have and keep you on track, helping your target audience get the results they want as quickly and meticulously as possible.

The Power of Mental Relaxation

Okay so, here's what I want you to do. I want you to find a comfortable chair that you can sit in and relax your mind as you take three calming breaths in.

Let your mind enter a state of relaxation and imagine yourself teaching what you know to someone else.

Again, remember that you don't have to know all of the steps up front because they will probably change after you arrange and rearrange the data and information that you're curating.

But for now, the goal is simply to imagine yourself teaching what you already know in a step-by-step framework that anyone can follow. Right now, I just want you to simply allow your intuitive mind to lead and guide you to come up with ideas about what it is that you actually do and how you do it.

Automatic Writing Exercise

Okay so, let's explore how the **Automatic Writing Exercise** can help you uncover what it is that you truly do.

This exercise is a powerful tool to access the subconscious, by passing overthinking and allowing your truest thoughts and feelings to flow freely onto the page. It works because it taps into the parts of you that already *know* your purpose, even if your conscious mind hasn't caught up yet.

Here's how it works:

1. **Set the Stage**: Find a quiet space where you won't be interrupted. Grab a pen and paper or open a blank document on your computer. Set a timer for 10 to 15 minutes.

2. **Start with a Prompt**: Begin with an open-ended question that invites exploration. For example:

   - "What do I do that truly impacts others?"
   - "How do I help people transform their lives?"
   - "What is my unique gift, and how do I share it?"

3. **Write Without Judgment**: As soon as you start, let the words flow without stopping to think, edit, or judge. The goal is to write whatever comes to mind, even if it seems random, repetitive, or unrelated. The magic lies in the stream of consciousness—it reveals insights that your logical mind might overlook.

4. **Look for Patterns and Themes**: Once your timer goes off, read through what you've written. Highlight words, phrases, or ideas that stand out. Pay attention to recurring themes or unexpected insights. Often, these are the breadcrumbs that will lead you to a deeper understanding of what it is that you do.

5. **Ask Why**: Take those key ideas and dig deeper. For example, if you wrote, "I help people find clarity," ask yourself why clarity matters and how you uniquely deliver it. This process refines your understanding of what you do and why it matters.

The beauty of automatic writing is that it bypasses your inner critic and brings forth truths you may not have consciously acknowledged. It's a tool for uncovering not just *what* you do, but *why* you do it and *how* you do it in a way that no one else can. The result? A clearer, more authentic understanding of your purpose and how you serve the world.

Reverse-Engineer Your "Identity Statement"

Okay so, another thing you can do is reverse engineer your "Identity Statement", or what some call your value proposition statement, by stepping into the shoes of your ideal client.

You want to picture that you've just delivered an amazing service or experience to your ideal client. And you want to imagine what they would say about you. Why? Because their words hold the key to confirming what you do best.

Start by asking yourself these reflective questions:

- *Why did this client choose me?*
- *What were the key factors that led them to work with me?*
- *How would they describe the value I brought to their life or business?*
- *What do they value most about working with me?*
- *What is the real, tangible, or intangible value I provide?*

These answers provide clarity, not just about what you do, but about how others perceive the unique impact of your work.

To sum it up, this chapter wasn't just about defining your work, it was about laying the foundation for something much deeper. It's about inspiring trust, standing out in your field, and aligning your actions with who you truly are at your core and who you're meant to serve. This process isn't just about finding clarity; it's about building confidence and creating a connection that resonates with the people who need you most.

In Chapter 2, you'll learn how to create a clear, compelling vision for your future—one that guides and motivates you to take purposeful action every day. This chapter focuses on defining what success looks like for you and building a vision that aligns with your deepest values and aspirations.

Here's what you'll learn:

- **The Power of Vision:** Understand why having a clear, powerful vision is essential for success and how it shapes your decisions, actions, and mindset.

- **Clarifying Your Purpose:** Learn how to identify what truly matters to you, so your vision is rooted in your deepest values and passions.

- **Visualizing Your Ideal Future:** Discover techniques to vividly imagine the life you want to create, from the big picture down to the small details.

- **Aligning Your Vision with Your Identity:** Learn how to craft a vision that reflects who you are at your core, ensuring that your goals are in harmony with your authentic self.

- **Setting Specific and Measurable Goals:** Break down your vision into concrete, achievable milestones that will move you closer to your ideal future.

- **Creating a Vision Statement:** Learn how to write a powerful vision statement that encapsulates your purpose, goals, and the impact you want to make.

- **Staying Motivated by Your Vision:** Discover strategies to keep your vision alive and inspiring, even when challenges arise, or progress feels slow.

By the end of this chapter, you'll have a crystal-clear vision for your future vision that will serve as a roadmap for your actions, decisions, and personal growth as you move toward the life you've always dreamed of.

CRAFTING YOUR VISION

"Vision without execution is a hallucination."

— *Thomas Edison*

Okay so, now that you have articulated what your "Identity Statement" is, and you've gained a better understanding of who you are and what it is that you actually do! Now it's time to come up with a vision for how you want your life to be. Why? Because part of turning your goals, dreams, and desires into reality comes down to you being clear about what it is that you actually want and then being clear about what it is you're committed to doing to make it happen. Am I Right?

Why? Because without a clear vision of what your life looks like, and feels like, it will be almost impossible to turn what you want into reality, because you're not fully committed to making it happen or because it seems unrealistic to you. And so, before you can truly turn what you want into reality, you must first have a clear vision of what it is, what it looks and feels like, and why you want it in the first place.

Why? Because the "Why" behind why you want what you want will drive you to take action on making it happen because when the going gets tough or when you feel like giving up, you won't because your "Why" will be driving you.

And so, the clearer you are about what it is that you want, the easier it will be for you to turn it into reality because you are fully committed to making it happen, no matter how long it takes. Am I Right?

Wishing Versus Receiving

And so, why? Because there's a big difference between wishing something would happen versus actually making it happen. And so, that's why Napoleon Hill, author of "Think and Grow Rich", wrote: "There is a difference between wishing for a thing and being ready to receive it." And why he also wrote that "No one is ready for a thing until he or she believes he or she can acquire it.

And so, before you can truly turn what you want into reality, you must first believe that it's possible, and then you must be fully committed to making it happen, no matter how long it takes. Why? Because if what you want for your life doesn't scare and excite you all at the same time, that means that you're not dreaming big enough.

Why? Because not only should your goals, dreams, and desires motivate and persuasive you to keep on going when the going gets tough, but it should also wake you up in the morning and keep you up late at night griding to make it happen. As Napoleon Hill also eloquently stated, 'Whatsoever the mind of man can conceive and believe, he can achieve.' Am I Right?

Creative Visualization

To transform your dreams into reality, the first step is to create a vivid and detailed picture of what you want—one that encompasses every aspect of your life. This isn't just about setting vague goals or aspirations. It's about painting a clear, compelling vision of your future, one that your mind can hold onto and begin to work toward.

Why is this so important? Because the clearer you are about what you want, the sooner your brain and subconscious mind will start aligning with that vision and help you bring it to life.

The reason clarity is so essential lies in the way your brain operates. Your mind cannot create something from nothing. It needs a reference point, a concrete image from which to begin its work.

This image is the blueprint that your brain will use to create the future you desire. Without it, the process stalls before it even begins.

When you articulate what you want in vivid detail, your brain forms a mental image of it and connects that image to the information it has already stored from past experiences, beliefs, and memories. This is how the mind processes everything.

Your brain operates through what is known as "mental associations." It takes the image of your desire and compares it to what is already in your mental repository.

Based on this comparison, it begins to make decisions and take actions that align with the life it believes you should be living. This is where the real power lies: your mind works not based on what is actually *true* in the world, but on what it perceives as true, based on the associations it has formed.

This is where phenomenology, a philosophical concept, comes into play. In simple terms, phenomenology asserts that we each experience the world through our own subjective lens. This lens is shaped by our perceptions, past experiences, and the mental constructs we've created.

And so, our personal sense of reality—the world we see and interact with—is not an objective truth, but a subjective reality we've built inside our minds. What does this mean for you? It means that your reality, the life you live, is not fixed. It's a creation, shaped by the way you see the world and yourself. And the most exciting part of all is that you have the power to change it.

Therefore, the version of reality you've been living up until now is just one interpretation, one possibility among many. You can reimagine it, reshape it, and create a new version of your life that aligns with your deepest desires. Now, this doesn't mean that the world outside of your mind is "not real."

What it means is that your brain and subconscious mind cannot distinguish between what's actually happening in the physical world and what you vividly imagine in your mind.

And so, once your brain begins to form a picture of what you want, it works as if that vision is already a part of your reality. Your thoughts, actions, and decisions all begin to align with that image, making it more likely that you will attract the circumstances, people, and opportunities necessary to bring it to fruition.

This is where the magic happens: when you become deeply clear about your vision when you describe it in full detail and believe in its possibility, your brain begins to treat that vision as a guiding principle, shaping your decisions and actions accordingly. The more real and tangible you make it in your mind, the more your mind will actively work toward it.

In other words, you're not just dreaming—you're building the foundation of your new reality. You're creating a frame of reference that guides every choice you make. And then your vision becomes the map, and your mind becomes the compass, directing you toward the life you've always dreamed of. The clearer your picture, the more powerful your subconscious mind becomes in helping you make that picture a reality.

So, take the time to craft your vision with precision and passion. Make it detailed. Make it bold. Make it something you can believe in. Because when you do, your mind will work tirelessly to bring that vision into existence. And then the world will begin to shift in response to the reality you've imagined. Your dream isn't just possible, it's inevitable.

Realistic, Achievable, Predictable and Sustainable (RAPS)

In the pursuit of your goals, dreams, and desires, one of the most critical steps is to ensure that the aspirations you set for yourself are realistic and achievable. It might seem intuitive, but too often, we set goals that are so ambitious they feel almost out of reach, and in doing so, we set ourselves up for failure before we even begin.

Why does this matter so much? Because when your goals feel too distant or unattainable, they can trigger an avalanche of self-doubt and negative thoughts. If you don't truly believe that your goals are possible, you'll begin to question your own abilities and wonder what, if anything, is achievable for you.

Over time, this disconnect between what you dream of and what you feel is possible could lead to frustration, disillusionment, and even despair. Instead of feeling motivated to take action, you start to feel stuck, as if you're running in circles—exerting effort without seeing any progress toward your destination.

When your goals seem impossible to reach, it's natural to search for distractions or detours that seem easier or more immediate. You might begin shifting focus to other things, trying to escape the deepening sense of disappointment that your original dreams feel too distant to ever become reality.

This ongoing struggle can slowly chip away at your self-confidence. Each failure, each unmet expectation, reinforces the belief that you're not capable of achieving anything significant. And as this cycle continues, you may begin to convince yourself that your dreams are simply unattainable. It becomes all too easy to settle for mediocrity, to tell yourself that maybe those dreams were never meant to be, when in fact, they were just set too high without a clear and achievable path to get there.

At this point, the stakes become even higher. If you remain trapped in this cycle, the very act of pursuing your dreams can feel like a relentless treadmill—one that burns up your energy and enthusiasm without ever getting you any closer to your destination. It's a dangerous pattern, one that leaves you feeling as if you're running against an invisible wall. And worse, it convinces you that the wall is permanent, that it can never be climbed, and that your aspirations were misguided from the start.

That's why ensuring that your goals are realistic isn't just a matter of avoiding frustration or failure. It's about creating a sustainable foundation for success—one that fuels your belief in yourself and the journey ahead. Why? Because by setting challenging goals that are within your reach, you not only set yourself up for incremental progress, but you also build a lasting sense of motivation, resilience, and self-assurance.

When your goals align with what you are truly capable of achieving, they shift from being daunting obstacles to valuable stepping stones. Each step forward brings you closer to your dream, reinforcing the belief that you are making progress.

The pursuit of your dreams becomes a rewarding process rather than a constant battle. With each achievable milestone, your confidence grows, and you develop the perseverance to continue on, even in the face of setbacks.

Ultimately, setting realistic goals isn't about aiming lower; it's about setting yourself up for a journey that keeps you inspired and moving forward, no matter what the challenges. It's about making your dreams feel tangible, possible, and within reach. When you believe in what you're capable of achieving, your goals cease to be sources of stress and self-doubt. They become the fuel that propels you forward, keeping your dreams alive and your spirit strong.

Make Sure Your Vision Is Achievable

Secondly, you must make sure they are achievable. Why? Because if you don't believe that you can achieve what you want in life, you set unrealistic goals for yourself that only lead to you having self-defeating thoughts about what you believe is really possible, which will then keep you stuck on a hamster wheel trying to do other things because the goals and dreams you've set for yourself are unrealistic and unachievable.

Why? Because your subconscious mind can only accept one truth at a time. Or as the late Henry Ford would say, "Whether you think you can, or you think you can't, you're right."

Why? Because your mind makes it so. And if you don't believe that it's possible, then you will never have the drive or motivation to make it happen.

So, that's why it needs to be achievable. Why? Because to make sure that your goals, dreams, and desires are achievable, you need to ask yourself:

- Does this goal stretch and challenge me to believe that it's possible?

- Do I have the knowledge, skills, and resources to accomplish it in a reasonable time, given your current situation?

- Are you prepared to keep going no matter the challenges or potential setbacks, no matter how long it takes?

If you answer "Yes" to any of these questions, then your goals, dreams, and desires have the possibility of becoming reality if you put in the work. But if your answer to any of these questions is "No", then it might just mean that your goals, dreams, and desires are not big enough or that you may need to think about how you can break them down into smaller more manageable goals.

Make Sure Your Vision is Predictable

In addition to being achievable, your goals should also be predictable. Why? Because predictability creates a sense of emotional attachment and certainty. When you know that a goal is attainable and that you have a clear path toward it, your subconscious mind becomes more committed to helping you make it happen. Why? Because your brain thrives on challenges, but it also needs clarity to direct its efforts toward success.

And so, to reaffirm what Henry Ford aptly put it, "Whether you think you can or you think you can't, you're right." This speaks to the power of belief. If your goals are unpredictable or seem too vague, it will be difficult to generate the focused energy needed to push them forward.

But when your vision is clear and well-defined, your mind will work tirelessly to align your actions with that vision, propelling you toward success.

Make Sure Your Vision is Sustainable

Lastly, for your goals, dreams, and desires to come to fruition, they must be sustainable. This is a pitfall that many entrepreneurs and ambitious individuals fall into: they become so overwhelmed by the enormity of what they want to achieve that they try to do it all alone. The belief that you must tackle everything yourself is a dangerous myth. Just like planning a long road trip, you wouldn't simply jump in the car and start driving without a map, preparation, or support along the way. Likewise, pursuing your dreams requires thoughtful planning and the right resources.

A sustainable vision allows for steady progress without burning you out or losing sight of your destination. It involves breaking down your larger goals into smaller, more manageable steps, and pacing yourself so that you don't run out of energy or motivation. Building a strong support system, whether through mentors, partners, or a network of friends and colleagues—is also essential.

Equally important is developing the knowledge and skills necessary to navigate your journey.

The Path to Success

The path to success is rarely linear. It will not always follow a straight line, and sometimes it may take unexpected turns. This is why flexibility is key. You must remain open to the journey as it unfolds, embracing whatever opportunities or challenges the universe brings your way. The road might look different than you initially imagined, but with persistence, resilience, and a well-thought-out plan, you'll still reach your destination—just perhaps in a way you didn't expect. In the end, pursuing your goals, dreams, and desires requires a combination of clarity, belief, and preparation.

When you set goals that are achievable, predictable, and sustainable, you create a foundation for success that keeps you motivated and focused, even through challenges. With the right mindset and a willingness to adapt, you can turn your dreams into reality.

Ultimately, the pursuit of your goals, dreams, and desires requires more than just ambition; it demands a well-rounded approach that combines clarity, belief, and strategy. When your goals are achievable, predictable, and sustainable, they become not just aspirations but guiding principles that steer you toward success. This foundation ensures that even when challenges arise, you remain grounded and focused on the bigger picture.

So, by setting goals that are within reach, you prevent the discouragement that comes from feeling overwhelmed or disillusioned. These goals become steppingstones, each one a tangible achievement that propels you forward. When your vision is predictable, you harness the power of your subconscious mind, which works tirelessly to align your thoughts and actions with your desired outcome. Your belief in what's possible becomes the catalyst for progress, fueling your drive and motivation.

And just as a long road trip requires careful planning and the right support, so too does the pursuit of your dreams. A sustainable vision means recognizing that success is a marathon, not a sprint. It's about pacing yourself, building a strong support system, and continuously learning and adapting along the way. The path may not always be smooth, and it may veer off course, but your ability to stay flexible and open to new opportunities will determine how far you can go.

In the end, it's about more than just reaching a destination. It's about crafting a journey that feels purposeful and fulfilling to you. And so, with the right mindset, a clear vision, and the necessary support, your dreams are not just possibilities, they are inevitable.

Choose One Goal

To begin, start by selecting one goal that you can realistically accomplish at this moment. Why? Because the primary reason most people fail to achieve the goals they set is that they attempt to tackle too many things at once, without giving any single goal their full, undivided attention. When your focus is scattered, your progress becomes diluted, making it harder to gain any real momentum.

In addition to ensuring your goals are realistic, achievable, predictable, and sustainable, they must also be **specific**. This is where many people go wrong. Simply saying, "I want to be happy," "I want to be successful," or "I want to be wealthy," is too vague. Specificity is key. It's not enough to wish for something—you must be clear about exactly what you want to create, how you plan to achieve it, and by when. Without this clarity, your goal lacks direction and purpose.

Don't wait for the "perfect" moment or for ideal conditions to present themselves. Success isn't about waiting for everything to align perfectly—it's about being proactive. Expect obstacles and challenges along the way and tackle each one as soon as they arise. The sooner you address problems, the faster you can move forward.

Write Your Own Goals

Now, it's time to put everything into action. Take a moment to **write down** your goal in clear, specific terms. For example, rather than saying, "I want to be more successful," say, "I will increase my business revenue by 25% within the next 6 months by launching a new marketing campaign."

Once you've defined your goal, follow this structure to create a roadmap for success:

1. **State the Goal**: What exactly do you want to accomplish? Make it specific and measurable.

2. **Action Plan**: What steps will you take to reach your goal? Break it down into smaller, manageable tasks.

3. **Target Date**: When do you want to achieve this goal? Set a realistic deadline to keep yourself accountable.

4. **Responsibility**: Who is responsible for each action? Are there tasks that require others to help or support you?

5. **Resources**: What resources—money, time, energy—are required to reach this goal? Be realistic about what you have and what you need.

6. **Results**: What will success look like? Define how you will measure your progress and ultimate achievement.

Once you've written your goals and outlined your action steps, prioritize them. Focus on the most important ones and tackle them first. Start with the first step, and don't let anything distract you from following through.

By focusing on one goal at a time, and by being specific and strategic, you will set yourself on a path to success.

The process might not always be easy, but with commitment and clarity, you will get closer to realizing your dreams. Now, go ahead—write your goals, create your action plan, and take that first step toward turning your vision into reality!

Goal/Action Plan

My ultimate goal is:

_____

_____

_____

_____

This is my ultimate target date:

_____

_____

_____

Here are the steps I will take to reach my goal, along with the target date for each:

1. _____

2. _____

3. _____

4. _____

The person responsible for each step is:

1. _____

2. _____

3. _____

4. _____

The money and time requirements are:

_____

_____

Here are the results:

_____

_____

Visualize The Process

Next, it's essential to visualize the process of what it will take to make your goals a reality. Why is this important? Because the more vivid you can create mental images of your desired outcomes, the sooner your brain will begin to form connections between what you want and how to bring it into existence. When you visualize, you strengthen the neurological pathways in your brain that are connected to the experiences you want to have, whether they are real or imagined.

The brain, as I've mentioned before, doesn't distinguish between what is real and what is imagined.

Its primary function is to produce the chemical compounds associated with your thoughts and feelings, and this ensures that you continue to think and feel in alignment with what you're visualizing. In other words, the act of visualization itself helps program your brain to believe in the possibility of your goal and sets you on the path to manifesting it in the real world.

Create a Mental Movie

So how do you start this process? Imagine you are creating a mental movie. Picture the people, places, and things you want to experience as part of your new reality. Why do we love movies? Because even though we know the characters on the screen are fictional, we still emotionally connect with their stories. Movies let us step into someone else's world and experience life through their eyes.

This is why they captivate us—they allow us to immerse ourselves in an alternate reality, one that we believe for a short time is real.

Now, to create the reality you desire, you must first produce a mental movie of that reality in your mind. You, the creator of your own life story, must imagine the scenes, the sounds, the emotions, and the details of the reality you're aiming to build. Just like any film, you are the writer, the director, and the actor. Before your desired future can unfold in the real world, it must first be constructed inside your head.

The Power of Mental Visualization

Why does this work? Everything you want to experience in life, whether it's success, health, wealth, relationships, or anything else, must first be created in your mind as a "mental movie." The brain processes everything through images, sounds, and feelings.

What we see, remember, and feel emotionally is the result of chemical reactions that occur in our brains. These mental experiences, whether they are based on reality or simply imagined, can be manipulated, edited, and refined with conscious awareness.

This ability to mentally rehearse and forecast future events is not just a whimsical idea; it's backed by research. We now know that we are not passive observers in life, we are active participants, constantly shaping our reality based on what we believe and visualize. The distinction between an "objective" reality and a "subjective" reality, one created in our minds, is blurry. We never experience anything that isn't already filtered through our perceptions, which means that the reality we live in is shaped by our thoughts and beliefs.

To create and experience the life you want, you must first experience it mentally. Picture yourself in the places, situations, and environments that align with your goals. Feel the emotions, hear the sounds, see the images—immerse yourself in that mental movie as though it's happening right now.

The Role of Cognitive Dissonance

Here's where it gets interesting. When you encounter something unfamiliar—something you've never experienced before—your mind will often create what is called "cognitive dissonance." This happens when your current beliefs or perceptions are challenged by new information. In essence, your mind struggles to reconcile this new idea with what it already knows to be true. Your body reacts to this dissonance as if it were "not true," because it lacks the frame of reference to understand it.

This is why, when you visualize a new reality for yourself, your mind might initially resist. It's hard to believe in something when there's no mental framework to support it.

However, by repeatedly engaging with your mental movie, you can condition your brain to accept this new reality. This is why you must visualize your future so vividly—that it feels like it is already happening.

Conditioning Your Brain and Body

The purpose of visualizing your desired reality is to condition your brain and body to experience that future ahead of time. The brain and body are incredibly adaptive, and they repeat patterns based on repetition. The more you mentally rehearse your desired life—living in places, experiencing the events, interacting with the people you envision—the more your brain and body will begin to believe that these things are already true.

In fact, the more you can immerse yourself in this mental movie, the more you'll activate the emotional centers of your brain. Emotions are the bridge between thought and action, and by emotionally engaging with your visualizations, you create a sense of belief and certainty that propels you forward. This belief is crucial because, once your brain and subconscious mind believe that what you are visualizing is happening now, they will begin to take actions that align with that belief.

The Trick: Believing It's Happening Now

The key is to convince your brain that what you're visualizing is not just a distant dream or a far-off future, it's happening **now**. When your brain and body believe that your goals are already in motion, you will feel more motivated, confident, and driven to take the necessary actions to bring them into reality. This process of mental rehearsal is powerful because it makes the impossible seem possible and the distant future feels immediate.

We already create mental movies in our heads constantly. We visualize our day ahead, plan conversations, or imagine what we'll have for dinner. What we often don't realize is that these mental images are creating the experiences we have in our lives. Whether you're planning a date or envisioning a job interview, you're already creating your future in your mind. Now, you can take that power and use it deliberately to create the life you truly want.

In conclusion, visualization is not just a motivational tool—it's a way to reprogram your brain and body to align with your goals. By creating a mental movie of the life, you want to live while emotionally engaging with it as if it's already happening, you set in motion the neural and emotional pathways that make it a reality. Your mind and body can't tell the difference between what's real and what's imagined, so why not imagine the life you desire and live it today, in your mind, before it happens in the world?

Brain Mapping Your Reality

The more you can visualize, imagine, and mentally rehearse being the person you aspire to be—doing the things you want to do with your life, the more your brain will create a mental map that aligns with these new experiences. This process is far more than a mere exercise in imagination; it's about reprogramming the brain to believe that these experiences are already a part of your reality.

Why is this so powerful? Because, deep within us, there exists an internal mental world—a complex network of brain cells that creates and maintains a map of both our body and the world around us. This map is continuously shaped by our thoughts, actions, and perceptions. By visualizing who you want to become and what you want to achieve, you are essentially rewiring your brain to reflect on these new goals and aspirations.

The Laws of Repetition and Association

This brings us to the laws of repetition and association. When we repeatedly expose our minds to new information—whether that information is real or imagined—we begin to create new neural connections associated with that experience. This process strengthens the brain's ability to make these connections, forming a new mental map that aligns with the vision we're creating. As the saying goes, "neurons that fire together, wire together."

Every thought, feeling, and memory is linked to a prior experience, and these memories carry emotional associations. This is why the act of visualizing is so powerful—because each thought you have is tied to an emotional response. When you imagine yourself living your ideal life, the brain recalls and activates those associated memories, which in turn triggers emotional reactions. This creates a cycle in which your thoughts influence your feelings, and your feelings then influence your actions. Over time, the more you mentally rehearse your desired reality, the more it becomes ingrained in your neural pathways.

The Chemistry of Change

Once these neural connections are activated, the brain's hypothalamus releases a chemical response that causes both the brain and body to act or react accordingly. Why is this important? Because every thought we have is connected to its own unique chemical signature. When you repeatedly think about your goals, dreams, and desires, your brain starts to produce the same chemicals that would be released if those experiences were already happening in real life. Essentially, you begin to biologically condition your body to act as though these imagined scenarios are already occurring.

This chemical feedback loop is crucial to achieving your goals because it fosters an internal state that mirrors the emotions and behaviors you would experience if your desired life were already in motion. As this process continues, your body becomes "addicted" to the emotions and feelings associated with your visualization.

In time, these mental rehearsals become automatic and habitual, creating a new default mode of thinking and behaving. Why? Because the body remembers what the mind forgets.

Chemical Addiction: The Power of Repetition

And so, the true power of visualization, imagination, and mental rehearsal lies in the ability to become biologically and chemically addicted to the thoughts, feelings, and behaviors that align with your desired reality. Just like a habit, the more you engage in this process, the more your brain and body will come to believe that this new reality is not just possible but inevitable. Over time, this process becomes a part of who you are, it becomes your default state of being.

Why does this matter? Because once your brain and body are convinced that your imagined reality is real, they will begin to act in ways that align with it. This means that the more you mentally rehearse being the person you want to become and living the life you want to live, the more your actions will mirror that vision.

In essence, you are training your mind and body to move towards your goals as if they are already within reach.

The Key: Your Imagination

At the core of this process is your imagination. Everything we experience, both directly and indirectly, is a result of what we imagine. One of the most fascinating aspects of the human brain is that it cannot distinguish between a vividly imagined scenario and a real-life experience. Both exist on the same energetic frequency.

And so, whether you're imagining success, health, wealth, or love, your brain and body react in much the same way as if those experiences were actually happening in the present moment.

This is why your imagination is such a powerful tool in the process of transformation. Why? Because when you visualize your desired outcomes, your brain activates the same neural networks and chemical reactions it would if those things were happening right now.

This is why successful athletes, entrepreneurs, and performers use visualization techniques to improve their performance, they're conditioning their minds and bodies to respond as though they've already succeeded.

Conditioning Your Brain and Body

Therefore, to make this process work for you, it's crucial to condition your brain and body every day. Each morning, set the intention to visualize the life you want to live, the person you want to become, and the experiences you want to have. Think about the people, places, and actions that align with your goals. Imagine yourself effortlessly achieving what you set out to do. As you continue to do this, it will become automatic. Just like muscle memory, your brain will "remember" how to think, feel, and act in alignment with your desired future.

By consistently repeating this process, you create a new habitual pattern in both your thoughts and behaviors. Over time, your mind and body will adopt these new patterns as the default, and the reality you've been imagining will begin to manifest in the physical world.

In conclusion, brain mapping your reality is a powerful tool for creating the life you desire. By using visualization, repetition, and association, you can rewire your brain to align with your goals.

The more you mentally rehearse your desired reality, the more you strengthen the neural pathways that will eventually bring it to life. Your imagination is not just a tool for creativity, it is the key to transforming your life. So, start today. Visualize the person you want to be, the life you want to live, and the world you want to create. Your brain and body are listening.

Craft Your Perfect Day

Okay so, imagine waking up every morning filled with purpose, knowing that every moment of your day aligns with the life you truly desire.

Most people drift through their days, caught in routines that neither inspire nor fulfill them, never stopping to ask a simple yet profound question: *Where is my life going?*

But what if you could design your life with intention, starting with just one perfect day? What would that day look like if fear, worry, and doubt was no longer part of the equation? What would you do, how would you feel, and who would you be if each day were lived as if it were your last?

Take a moment to reflect and imagine. Now, write it down. Craft your perfect day, step by step, from sunrise to sunset.

An Example of a Perfect Day

Here's a vision to inspire you:

- **6:00 AM:** Wake up and savor a cup of coffee, embracing the quiet stillness of the morning.

- **6:30 AM:** Spend 30 minutes to an hour immersed in a book that expands your mind or fuels your soul.

- **8:00 AM:** Enjoy a nourishing breakfast that energizes you for the day ahead.

- **8:30 AM:** Engage in 30 minutes of exercise to awaken your body and boost your vitality.

- **9:00 AM:** Meditate for 20 minutes, centering your mind and setting your intention for the day.

- **9:30 AM - 3:30 PM:** Dedicate 4-6 hours to work that fulfills you—whether it's creating, teaching, solving problems, or serving others.

- **4:00 PM:** Spend quality time with family or friends, building connections that matter.

- **7:00 PM:** Reflect on the day's lessons and victories for 20 minutes.

- **Evening:** Unwind with an activity you love and fall asleep with a grateful heart, knowing you lived fully.

Make your version of a perfect day uniquely yours. Think big, dream freely, and don't hold back.

Dream Big: The Power of Vision

Why? Because as Walt Disney famously said, *"All our dreams can come true if we have the courage to pursue them."* Your dreams are not mere fantasies; they are the seeds of your future reality. When you dare to dream big, you create a vision that inspires and challenges you to grow. If your dreams don't scare you, they're too small. Why? Because growth happens outside your comfort zone, where the seemingly impossible becomes achievable. Dreaming big therefore pushes your subconscious mind to rise to the challenge and unlock hidden potential.

Align Your Vision with Your Values

Your vision must not only inspire you but also resonate deeply with your core values. Why? Because misaligned goals create inner conflict and drain your motivation. For instance, if your vision demands excessive time away from your family, yet family is one of your core values, you may feel torn and unfulfilled.

Instead, refine your vision so it complements your values. This alignment ensures that your journey is not only successful but also authentic and meaningful. When your dreams honor what matters most to you, they become a source of joy, not sacrifice.

Cultivate a Positive Mindset

On the road to achieving your vision, you will face obstacles. That's inevitable.

But how you respond to these challenges will determine your success. A positive mindset transforms setbacks into steppingstones and failures into lessons.

Choose to see every situation—no matter how difficult—as an opportunity to grow. Focus on what's working, not what's broken. Optimism isn't about ignoring challenges; it's about facing them with resilience and hope.

Take Consistent Action

A vision without action is merely a dream. Success comes from committing to daily, intentional steps toward your goal. Remember, Rome wasn't built in a day, and neither will your vision. Think of progress as a snowball rolling down a hill. It starts small but gathers momentum with every push. Over time, those small, consistent actions compound into significant results.

Celebrate Your Milestones

Don't wait until you've reached the finish line to celebrate. Every milestone, no matter how small, deserves recognition.

Celebrating your progress reinforces your efforts and keeps you motivated for the journey ahead. Each step forward is a testament to your dedication and a reminder that you are capable of achieving greatness.

The Journey of Vision Creation

Creating a vision is a transformative process. It's about defining the life you want to live and taking deliberate steps to make it a reality. It's about dreaming big, staying aligned with your values, and cultivating a mindset that sees challenges as opportunities.

As you embark on this journey, remember that every great accomplishment starts with a single step. So, dream boldly, take consistent action, and cherish the process. Your ideal life is waiting—start designing it today.

Create a Realistic Back Story

To create the life you desire, you must first create a story—*your* story. Why? Because crafting a realistic backstory is not just an imaginative exercise; it's a powerful tool for conditioning your subconscious mind to experience your future reality as if it has already happened.

Think of it as starting with the end in mind, imagining the ideal version of yourself and your accomplishments, and then reverse-engineering the steps to get there. This process bridges the gap between your vision and the psychological motivation that drives it, grounding your aspirations in purpose and clarity.

The Power of Your Backstory

Your backstory serves as the foundation for the future you are building. It connects your vision with the "why" behind it—the deep-seated reasons that inspire and sustain you through challenges. For example, my own journey is fueled by a singular ambition: to become the #1 transformational speaker trainer in the world.

Why did I choose this path? Like many of you, I've wrestled with the frustration of seeing others—who seemed no more talented or gifted than me—achieve success while I sat on the sidelines, held back by my own doubts, fears, and insecurities.

This frustration lit a fire within me, sparking a journey of self-mastery and discovery. I immersed myself in learning, growing, and unlocking my full potential. But more importantly, I decided to take back control of my life and consciously create a reality that I believed was truly worth living.

A Vision Brought to Life

From that decision, everything changed. I went on to write five bestselling books and founded a coaching and training program designed to help aspiring speakers transform their stories into powerful messages. My work has been featured in *Forbes*, I delivered a TEDx talk, and I've spoken on hundreds of stages, teaching others how to unleash their best selves.

But let me be clear—this was not how my life began. Like so many others, I grappled with low self-esteem, a lack of confidence, and the nagging question: *Who am I, and what am I meant to do with my life?* The turning point came when I confronted what I now call a self-identity crisis. It was only through embracing this struggle—facing my doubts and fears head-on—that I began to understand who I truly was. I discovered my purpose and my potential, and from that place of clarity, I began to rise.

From Struggle to Purpose

Overcoming my inner turmoil wasn't easy, but it was necessary. Through this process, I shed limiting beliefs that no longer served me, silenced the voice of fear, and replaced it with one of courage and conviction.

This journey led me to my mission: to guide others through their own transformations. My purpose is to help people discover their voice, hone their message, and speak their truth with power and authority. Whether they take the stage or simply step into their lives with more confidence, I want to help them become the person they've always known they were meant to be.

Your Backstory Is Your Foundation

Now, it's your turn. Creating a backstory isn't about fabricating an idealized version of yourself; it's about *futurizing* your life. It's about imagining the version of you who has achieved everything you desire and reflecting on the struggles and triumphs that brought you there.

Ask yourself:

- Who do I want to become?
- What legacy do I want to leave?
- What challenges did I overcome to get here?

The answers to these questions will shape the blueprint of your backstory. Once you've written it, revisit it often. Let it fuel your subconscious mind, conditioning it to believe in the reality of your vision. When you see yourself as a person who has already achieved success, you begin to align your actions, decisions, and habits with that version of yourself.

Reverse-Engineering Your Vision

After crafting your backstory, the next step is to reverse-engineer it. Break down the vision into actionable steps. Are your current actions, thoughts, and behaviors aligned with the future you want to create? If not, adjust them.

Remember: the life you envision isn't built overnight. It's constructed through small, consistent efforts compounded over time.

Every decision, every habit, every intentional step brings you closer to the version of yourself you've written into your backstory.

A Life Worth Living

My story didn't begin with bestselling books, standing ovations, or global recognition.

It began with frustration, doubt, and a deep longing for more. The transformation happened when I chose to take responsibility for my life and shape it into something meaningful.

Now, my mission is clear: to inspire, guide, and empower others to write their own stories, find their voice, and step into their greatness. Because I believe that every one of us has a message worth sharing, a life worth living, and a purpose worth pursuing.

Why Create a Backstory?

A backstory serves as the foundation for your personal and professional identity. It connects your vision of the future with your present reality, acting as a bridge between who you are now and who you aspire to become. By crafting a compelling backstory, you condition your subconscious mind to see your goals and dreams as achievable realities. It's not just an imaginative exercise, it's a psychological strategy that aligns your actions, decisions, and mindset with your ideal self.

When you clearly define your backstory, you create a powerful narrative that fuels motivation and builds resilience. It helps you stay focused, overcome doubts, and navigate challenges because you've already visualized the life, you're committed to creating. Your backstory anchors you to your purpose, providing clarity and a sense of direction.

How to Create Your Backstory in Chronological Order

Step 1: Define Your End Goal

Start by imagining your ideal future. Envision the life you've always dreamed of, where you've accomplished your goals and are living your purpose. Think of this as the final chapter in your story.

- **Questions to ask yourself:**
    - Who am I in this ideal future?

- What have I achieved?
- How do I feel, and what is my daily life like?

Write down these details vividly. The clearer your vision, the more powerful your backstory will be.

Step 2: Identify Your Identity Statement

From your envisioned future, craft an *Identity Statement*—a single, powerful declaration of who you are at your core and what you stand for. This statement defines the role you're committing to play in life and serves as the anchor for your backstory.

For example,

"I am a transformational leader who inspires others to find their voice and create meaningful change in their lives."

Step 3: Work Backward to Identify Key Milestones

Now, reverse-engineer your journey. Start from the future and outline the major milestones that would logically lead to your end goal. Think of these as the steppingstones that brought you to your ideal life.

For example:

- You became a sought-after speaker, sharing your message on global stages.
- You launched a bestselling book that resonated with thousands.
- You overcame personal challenges like self-doubt, fear, or financial struggles.

These milestones give your backstory a sense of progression and authenticity.

Step 4: Describe Your Starting Point

Every great backstory begins with a humble or challenging starting point. Reflect on where you are today and the struggles, doubts, or obstacles you've faced. This creates a sense of relatability and shows your growth over time.

For example:

- "I started as someone unsure of my purpose, struggling with self-doubt and searching for clarity."

Your starting point sets the stage for the transformation that follows.

Step 5: Fill in the Journey with Specific Steps and Experiences

Outline the key actions, decisions, and moments that shaped your path. This is the core of your backstory, the journey from where you started to where you are going. Be detailed and specific.

For example:

- You invested time in self-development, reading, and learning from mentors.
- You joined workshops or training programs that helped you hone your skills.
- You experienced setbacks but learned critical lessons that shaped your perspective.
- You celebrated small wins along the way, building momentum toward your goals.

Step 6: Validate Your Role

As you craft your backstory, ensure that the role you've envisioned aligns with your values, passions, and strengths.

- **Ask yourself:**
    - Does this version of me feel authentic?
    - Are my actions and decisions consistent with the person I want to become?

This step ensures that your backstory feels realistic and connected to your true self.

Step 7: Immerse Yourself in the Vision

Bring your backstory to life by imagining specific scenes from your future. Picture yourself in action—whether it's giving a keynote speech, signing copies of your bestselling book, or mentoring others to achieve their dreams. Feel the emotions tied to these moments.

For example:

- "I stood on stage, looking out at a sea of inspired faces, knowing I had changed lives."

The more vividly you can see and feel these experiences, the more your subconscious mind will work to make them real.

Step 8: Reinforce Your Backstory Daily

Your backstory is not a one-time exercise. Revisit it regularly and internalize it through visualization, journaling, or affirmations. By repeatedly focusing on your backstory, you'll strengthen your belief in the reality you're creating.

For example:

- Every morning, visualize yourself living your ideal life.
- Write affirmations that reflect your Identity Statement.

Final Thoughts

Your backstory is your compass, guiding you toward your ideal future. By crafting it in a chronological, step-by-step manner, you create a narrative that inspires and motivates you to take intentional actions. Remember, the power of your backstory lies in its ability to bridge the gap between who you are now and who you're becoming. Take the time to craft it with care, it's the foundation of the life you're building.

In Chapter 3, *Reverse Engineering Your Vision,* you will learn how to take the future you've envisioned and break it down into actionable steps. This chapter is about working backward from your goals to map out a clear and intentional path to success.

Here's what you can expect to dive into:

- **Clarifying the Big Picture:** Learn how to vividly define your ultimate vision—what your ideal life looks like, how you want to feel, who you want to serve, and the impact you want to make.

- **Identifying Milestones:** Discover how to pinpoint the key markers along the way that indicate you're on the right track.

- **Breaking It Down:** Get practical strategies for turning long-term aspirations into smaller, manageable tasks that align with your core identity and purpose.

- **Reassessing and Refining:** Understand the importance of flexibility and recalibrating your plan as life evolves, ensuring your actions always align with your larger vision.

By the end of this chapter, you'll have a clear, actionable framework to start turning your dreams into reality—one deliberate step at a time.

3

REVERSE ENGINEERING YOUR VISION

"Success is not a matter of chance, it's a matter of choice. Reverse engineer your vision and work backwards to create the future you desire."

— *Unknown*

Did you know that your brain has an extraordinary skill? When you tell it to look for something, it tends to find it. Whether it's an opportunity, a person, or even a solution to a problem, your brain will focus on what you direct it towards. Why? Because when you can clearly define what you want, your brain will naturally start aligning your thoughts, actions, and perceptions to help you get it.

And so, when you understand that your life is not set in stone and that it is malleable, changeable, and can be molded and shaped into whatever you desire — you will start to see how to break it down into manageable, simple steps. And so, by the end of this chapter, my goal is to show you how to take your vision, no matter how big or grand it is, and break it down into actionable, manageable steps.

Start with the End in Mind

Okay so, before you can reverse engineer your life into what you want, you first need to know where you're going. Why? Because the power to create the life you want begins with a clear vision, a solid plan, and the commitment to take consistent action daily.

And so, you need to imagine your life as a journey and that your vision is the map. Why? Because your vision isn't something you wait for; it's something you intentionally create.

Don't worry about whether it's realistic or not. Just start with a bold vision. The clearer and more specific you can make it, the easier it will be to work backward to turn it into reality. So, take some time right now to reflect and get clear on what you want.

Reverse Engineering Your Vision Through Who You Are Becoming

Imagine this: you have a dream, a vision for your life. You want to become a successful entrepreneur, a healthy individual, a loving partner, or perhaps someone who enjoys financial freedom. But how do you turn this vision into reality? The answer lies in one powerful concept: **reverse engineering** your life based on **who you declare yourself to be.**

Why? Because the person you are becoming — your identity — is the key to unlocking your dreams. Once you identify **who you are becoming**, reverse engineering your vision becomes the process of aligning your actions with this identity.

The Power of Your "I Am" Statement

Before you start breaking down your vision into steps, let us take a moment to reflect back on your "Identity Statement."

Why? Because **who are you becoming?** Your "Identity Statement," is more than just words; it is the person you have declared yourself to be that will shape your mindset and drive the actions and decisions you make. For example, if your "Identity Statement" is that you're a successful innovative entrepreneur, then your vision might be to create a thriving business that impacts your industry.

The key is to **align** your vision with who you are becoming. Why? Because when your vision is aligned with the person you have declared yourself to be, it will become a reflection of your true authentic self.

And when you create goals that resonate with your true authentic self, you feel more connected to your vision, making it that much easier to stay focused and motivated on achieving it.

Set Milestones Checkpoints

Next, you want to set milestones and checkpoints. Why? Because setting milestones will help you maintain momentum and help stay focused on the bigger picture. Milestones act as small wins that build momentum and confidence, making the larger goal seem more possible to achieve. Each milestone is a mini-goal that leads you closer to your larger vision, and helps you celebrate along the way.

The Neuroscience Behind Reverse Engineering

Reverse engineering is a powerful approach to achieving your goals because it leverages the natural workings of your brain, specifically the **Reticular Activating System (RAS)**. The RAS acts as a gatekeeper for your brain, filtering information and determining what gets your attention.

When you define a clear goal and visualize the steps backward from its completion, your RAS activates to focus your awareness on the resources, opportunities, and solutions that align with your vision. Think of the RAS as a radar system, constantly scanning your environment to prioritize what's relevant to your objectives.

For instance, if you've ever decided to buy a particular car and suddenly started seeing that model everywhere, that's your RAS at work. It didn't manifest the cars—they were always there. But now, your brain has been primed to notice them. Similarly, when you reverse-engineer a goal, your RAS works to identify the tools, people, and strategies that will help you achieve it.

The key is specificity. The clearer and more detailed your vision, the more effectively your brain will focus on identifying the necessary steps.

Vague goals result in vague progress. Precise goals activate the RAS like a magnet, pulling you closer to your desired reality.

Adaptation and Flexibility: Adjusting Your Plan

While reverse engineering provides a structured path, it's important to acknowledge that life is dynamic. Challenges, unexpected changes, and new opportunities will arise, and your ability to adapt is critical.

Flexibility doesn't mean abandoning your vision—it means reassessing your steps and strategies when necessary.

How to Stay Flexible While Reverse Engineering:

1. Reassess Regularly:

Periodically revisit your goals and milestones. Are they still relevant? Are they aligned with your evolving circumstances and values?

2. Embrace Challenges as Opportunities:

When obstacles appear, view them as opportunities to learn, grow, or pivot. Often, these challenges reveal new pathways you hadn't considered.

3. Update Your Milestones:

Adjust your timelines or redefine intermediate goals to reflect what you've learned along the way. For instance, a delay in one area might uncover new skills or connections that ultimately accelerate progress in another.

4. Stay Focused on the Big Picture:

Even as you adjust the details, keep your larger vision intact. Adaptation is about finding new ways to move forward and not giving up on where you want to go.

Reverse Engineering as a Living Process

Think of reverse engineering as a *living framework* rather than a fixed plan.

Your path may evolve as you gain new insights and encounter unexpected events. Growth and learning are part of the journey, and your flexibility allows you to respond creatively to whatever comes your way.

By combining the power of your RAS with the adaptability to navigate life's uncertainties, you create a system that keeps you moving toward your goals—regardless of the challenges.

Reverse engineering, when done with clarity and flexibility, becomes not only a method for achieving success but also a mindset for thriving in an ever-changing world.

Putting It All Together: The Steps to Reverse Engineering Your Vision

Reverse engineering your vision is about transforming dreams into reality by breaking them into manageable, actionable steps. Here's how to do it effectively:

1. Clarify Your End Goal

Start by vividly imagining your ideal life. What does success look and feel like? Consider the values you want to uphold, the impact you wish to make, and the kind of fulfillment you desire. The clearer and more detailed your end goal, the easier it becomes to map out your journey.

2. Break It Down into Key Areas

Divide your vision into distinct areas of life that matter most to you. These might include:

- **Career/Business:** What achievements or roles define success for you?

- **Health:** What does optimal physical and mental well-being look like?

- **Relationships:** How do you envision your relationships with family, friends, or a partner?

- **Finances:** What financial stability or abundance do you aspire to?

- **Personal Growth:** What skills, habits, or qualities do you want to cultivate?

Breaking your vision into these areas makes the process feel less overwhelming and more focused.

3. Set Long-Term Goals

For each key area, establish specific, measurable goals that align with your vision. For example:

- In your **career**, your long-term goal might be to "Become a thought leader in my industry."

- In **health**, it might be "Run a marathon in two years."

These goals become the pillars that support your larger vision.

4. Create Milestones

Break your long-term goals into smaller, actionable milestones. These are the steppingstones that keep you on track and provide a sense of progress. For instance:

- To "become a thought leader," milestones might include writing articles, networking with industry leaders, or speaking at events.

- To "run a marathon," milestones could include running a 5K, then a 10K, before building up to a full marathon.

These smaller achievements build momentum and keep your motivation high.

5. Develop Daily Habits

Consistent action is the foundation of success. Identify the daily habits that will lead to your milestones and integrate them into your routine.

- If your goal is career advancement, daily habits might include reading industry news or practicing public speaking.

- For health, it might mean a morning jog or meal prepping for the week.

These small, consistent steps compound over time, bringing you closer to your vision.

6. Stay Flexible

Life is unpredictable, and your journey may not always follow the exact path you've mapped out. Unexpected challenges or opportunities might require you to adapt your strategy. Flexibility allows you to pivot without losing sight of your ultimate goal.

- Reassess your goals periodically to ensure they still align with your vision and circumstances.

- Treat setbacks as opportunities to learn and grow, not reasons to abandon your vision.

7. Celebrate Progress

Each milestone achieved is a victory worth celebrating.

These moments of acknowledgment provide motivation and remind you of how far you've come. Reward yourself in ways that align with your goals, reinforcing your commitment to the process.

Reverse Engineering in Action

Reverse engineering is a systematic way to transform your aspirations into reality. By starting with the end in mind and working backward, you create a roadmap that leads directly to the life you want.

This process is not about perfection but about consistent progress. With a clear vision, actionable steps, and the right mindset, success isn't just possible, it's inevitable.

Remember, the journey will have ups and downs, but the key is to stay committed to the process. Show up every day, take one step closer, and trust in your ability to build the future you've envisioned.

Your dreams are within reach, and with this blueprint, you have everything you need to bring them to life.

In Chapter 4, *Turn Your Vision into a To-Do List,* you'll learn how to transform your grand vision into a practical, actionable plan that keeps you moving forward every single day. This chapter is where strategy meets execution.

Here's what you'll gain from this chapter:

- **Prioritization for Progress:** Learn how to identify the most critical tasks that will have the greatest impact on your goals and ensure they align with your long-term vision.

- **The Power of Micro-Steps:** Discover how to break larger goals into bite-sized, daily actions that feel manageable and keep momentum alive.

- **Time-Blocking Your Life:** Explore methods to organize your schedule in a way that prioritizes what matters most, making time for your vision without feeling overwhelmed.

- **Overcoming Procrastination:** Equip yourself with tools and techniques to stay motivated, overcome resistance, and take consistent action—even when the path feels daunting.

- **Tracking Your Wins:** Develop a system to measure progress, celebrate milestones, and adjust your to-do list as needed to stay on track.

By the end of this chapter, you'll have a clear and actionable daily plan that connects your big-picture vision to the steps you take today, ensuring your dream life is built one task at a time.

TURN YOUR VISION INTO A TO-DO-LIST

"A vision without a plan is just a dream. Turn your vision into a to-do list, and watch your dreams come to life, one task at a time."

— *Unknown*

Mastering Your Goals Through the Power of a To-Do List.

One of the greatest obstacles to achieving your goals, dreams, and desires is the feeling of being overwhelmed by everything on your plate. It's that crushing weight of endless tasks that can leave you paralyzed, unsure of where to start. This is where the power of a well-crafted to-do list comes in—a simple yet profoundly effective tool to help you organize, prioritize, and take control of your day.

The Science Behind a To-Do List

Why does a to-do list work so well? Neuroscience provides the answer. Research shows that when we organize and prioritize our tasks, it reduces mental clutter and creates a sense of clarity. This act of planning not only makes the workload feel more manageable but also frees the mind from the stress of trying to remember everything.

Checking off tasks as you complete them is more than just satisfying; it releases dopamine, the "feel-good" neurotransmitter. This natural boost in dopamine reinforces productivity and motivates you to keep moving forward.

Your to-do list, then, is more than a tool—it's a strategy to increase focus, reduce stress, and create a steady momentum toward your goals.

Step 1: Understand the Purpose of Your To-Do List

A to-do list is not about overwhelming yourself with everything you could possibly do. Its purpose is to *simplify* your day by helping you focus on what you can realistically achieve right now. Think of it as your partner, guiding you through your day, not a dictator controlling your every move.

Step 2: Limit Your List to Seven Items

The human brain struggles to juggle more than seven pieces of information at a time. This limitation, known as *Miller's Law*, is why phone numbers typically have seven digits. When your list grows too long, it becomes counterproductive, leaving you feeling overwhelmed rather than empowered.

To stay productive, focus on a maximum of seven tasks at a time. This keeps your workload manageable and ensures you stay clear-headed and motivated.

Step 3: Prioritize Your Tasks

Deciding which task to tackle first is a critical step in taking control of your day. Start by identifying tasks that:

- Align with your highest priorities.
- Have immediate deadlines.
- Will create a ripple effect of progress once completed.

By doing this, you eliminate decision fatigue and direct your energy toward what truly matters.

Step 4: Break It Down Into Milestones

Large tasks can feel daunting, so break them into smaller, actionable steps. For example:

- Instead of "Write a book," break it down into:
    1. Create an outline.
    2. Write the introduction.
    3. Draft one chapter.

Each milestone brings a sense of accomplishment, building momentum as you move closer to completing the larger goal.

Step 5: Check Off and Celebrate Progress

As you check off items on your list, you're not just getting things done—you're also building confidence and reinforcing positive habits. This act sends a powerful signal to your brain: *I'm making progress.*

Take a moment to celebrate each small win, whether it's finishing a task, completing a milestone, or even just sticking to your plan for the day.

Step 6: Stay Flexible and Reassess

Life is unpredictable. As circumstances change, so too should your to-do list. Reassess your priorities as needed, and don't be afraid to move lower-priority tasks to another day. Flexibility ensures that your list serves you—not the other way around.

Why It Works

When used effectively, a to-do list becomes more than a productivity hack—it becomes a tool for clarity, focus, and mental well-being. It helps you move from a state of overwhelm to a place of calm, intentional action.

The process of creating, prioritizing, and completing tasks aligns your efforts with your goals, keeping you on track and motivated. And the best part? Each step you take builds momentum, bringing you closer to the life you're working so hard to create.

Remember: Your to-do list is a reflection of your intentions for the day. Keep it simple, focused, and flexible. With the right mindset and approach, it's a small habit that can lead to massive results.

Putting It All Together

Before tackling any task, take a few moments to evaluate and plan. This strategic pause allows you to focus on what's important, delegate what's not, and approach your work with clarity and purpose.

By prioritizing tasks, assessing their validity, clarifying objectives, outsourcing strategically, planning effectively, and setting deadlines, you create a system that maximizes your time and energy.

Incorporating these steps into your daily routine will not only reduce stress but also ensure that every action you take moves you closer to your goals. Remember: success isn't about doing everything—it's about doing the right things.

Step 1: Prioritize Your Task

Before diving into any task, pause and ask yourself the following questions:

- *If I could do only one thing today, which task would have the greatest impact on my goals?*
- *Will this task move me closer to my desired outcome?*

- *Do I really need to do this task right now, or can it be delegated or delayed?*

By focusing on priorities, you train yourself to keep your eyes on the big picture.

This prevents you from wasting time on tasks that don't align with your overall strategy. Remember, losing perspective is the fastest way to derail your progress.

Step 2: Assess the Validity of Your Task

Not every task on your list deserves your immediate attention—or your attention at all. To determine whether a task is worth doing, ask yourself:

- *What would happen if I delayed this task for a week, a month, or even forever?*
- *Does this task excite and motivate me, or am I avoiding something more important?*

Focusing on tasks you're passionate about or that have tangible importance will keep you energized and productive. Avoid wasting time on activities that don't align with your goals or that serve as distractions.

Step 3: Clarify What Needs to Be Done

Ambiguity can stall progress, so always define your task clearly before starting. Ask yourself:

- *What exactly do I need to accomplish?*
- *What does the finished product look like?*
- *What outcome am I working toward?*

The more specific you are, the better you can streamline your approach. This clarity allows you to move forward with confidence and ensures your efforts yield meaningful results.

Step 4: Decide If You Should Be Doing It

Here's a productivity secret: You don't have to do everything yourself. Evaluate whether a task is the best use of your time and energy. Ask yourself:

- *Is this task really worth my time?*
- *Can someone else do this better or faster than I can?*
- *Would outsourcing this task free up my time for higher-value activities?*

Outsource tasks that don't align with your strengths, and focus your efforts on what you do best. Remember, your time is more valuable than money—use resources wisely to maximize your productivity.

Step 5: Find the Most Effective Approach

Abraham Lincoln famously said, *"Give me six hours to chop down a tree, and I will spend the first four sharpening the ax."* Preparation is key. Take a moment to identify the most efficient way to tackle your task. Consider:

- *What tools, resources, or people can help me complete this task efficiently?*
- *Are there any skills I need to learn or improve to execute this task effectively?*

Investing time upfront to strategize will save you hours of frustration and effort in the long run.

Step 6: Assign a Deadline

Deadlines are powerful motivators. They create a sense of urgency, encourage focus, and help you stay organized. To make the most of this strategy:

- Set realistic deadlines for every task, no matter how small.

- Break larger tasks into smaller chunks, each with its own deadline.

Studies show that deadlines not only boost performance but also help you prioritize what matters most. Writing them down reinforces your commitment to completing the task.

In Chapter 5, you'll learn how to tap into the immense power of your subconscious mind to rewire your thoughts, beliefs, and behaviors for success.

This chapter will teach you how to reprogram your brain, remove limiting beliefs, and install new patterns of thought that align with your vision.

Here's what you'll learn:

- **The Power of the Subconscious Mind:** Understand how the subconscious mind influences your actions, decisions, and outcomes, often without your conscious awareness.

- **Rewriting Limiting Beliefs:** Learn how to identify and release limiting beliefs that hold you back, replacing them with empowering thoughts that support your goals.

- **The Science of Neuroplasticity:** Discover how your brain can change and adapt throughout your life, allowing you to form new neural pathways and behaviors.

- **Visualization Techniques:** Master the art of visualization to imprint your desired outcomes on your subconscious mind, making your goals feel more attainable.

- **Using Affirmations for Reprogramming:** Learn how to craft and use powerful affirmations to shift your mindset and reinforce your new beliefs.

- **Creating Positive Mental Habits:** Discover practical strategies to create new, positive habits that support your success and align with your vision.

- **The Power of Consistency:** Understand why repetition is key to reprogramming your brain and how consistent mental training leads to lasting change.

By the end of this chapter, you'll have the tools and knowledge to harness the power of your subconscious mind, break free from old patterns, and reprogram your brain to support your journey toward success.

5

PROGRAMMING YOUR BRAIN AND SUBCONSCIOUS MIND

"Your subconscious mind is the greatest power you possess. Program it wisely and watch your life transform."

— *Unknown*

A Guide to Aligning Your Inner World with Your Goals.

Okay so, now that you've mapped out your vision, broken it into actionable steps, and prioritized your to-do list, it's time to take things to the next level. This involves programming your brain and subconscious mind to work in alignment with your goals, making your desired thoughts and actions automatic and habitual.

The Science Behind Subconscious Programming

Imagine learning to ride a bike or play a new instrument. In the beginning, your conscious mind does all the heavy lifting—processing every movement and detail. Over time, as you practice, the task becomes second nature, and your subconscious takes over.

The same principle applies to achieving your goals. However, before your brain and subconscious mind fully commit to helping you realize your dreams, you must first address a crucial element: the **Reticular Activating System (RAS).**

Understanding the Gatekeeper: Your Reticular Activating System (RAS)

The RAS is a sophisticated filtering mechanism within your brain, designed to sort through vast amounts of data and focus your attention on what aligns with your identity, beliefs, and priorities. Its primary function is to ensure that you perceive and act upon information that matches your self-perception and belief system while ignoring anything contradictory.

For instance, if you've subconsciously declared yourself as someone who "always struggles to succeed," your RAS will filter out opportunities and solutions that contradict this identity. Conversely, if you believe and affirm yourself as capable, resourceful, and destined for success, your RAS will prioritize and amplify the information and opportunities that align with this belief.

The Power of Alignment

Here's the critical takeaway: if your self-perception and beliefs are not in harmony with the goals you've set, your RAS will block you from taking action or even recognizing opportunities.

This is why aligning your conscious goals with your subconscious beliefs is non-negotiable. Your brain operates on a binary system—it either believes something is true and acts accordingly, or it doesn't believe it, and your progress stalls. There's no middle ground.

Bridging the Gap: Aligning Beliefs with Goals

To successfully program your brain and subconscious mind, you must create a strong, unified belief system that connects:

1. **Your current reality** (where you are now).

2. **Your desired destination** (the vision you want to achieve).

This alignment allows your RAS to make meaningful connections between the two, signaling your brain to take actionable steps toward your goals.

Steps to Program Your Brain and Subconscious Mind

1. Define Your Identity Statement

Start by crafting an identity statement that clearly reflects who you want to become. For example:

- Instead of saying, "I want to be successful," declare, "I am successful because I take consistent, focused action."

This shift establishes a foundation for your RAS to filter and accept information that supports this new identity.

2. Visualize with Clarity and Emotion

Visualization isn't just about imagining your goals; it's about experiencing them emotionally.

- Close your eyes and picture your desired outcome in vivid detail.
- Imagine the sights, sounds, feelings, and even the smells associated with your success.

When you attach strong emotions to your visualization, your brain perceives it as a lived experience, reinforcing your belief in its attainability.

3. Practice Affirmations Daily

Affirmations are powerful tools for reprogramming your subconscious. Use clear, present-tense statements like:

- "I am resourceful and capable of achieving my goals."
- "I attract opportunities that align with my vision."

Repeat these affirmations consistently, especially during moments of quiet focus, such as in the morning or before bed.

4. Rewire Limiting Beliefs

Identify and challenge any beliefs that contradict your goals. Ask yourself:

- What evidence do I have that this belief is true?
- How does this belief serve me?

Replace limiting beliefs with empowering ones, and reinforce them through action.

5. Take Aligned Action

Beliefs without action are meaningless. To solidify the programming of your RAS and subconscious mind, take steps—no matter how small—that align with your new identity. Each action reinforces the message to your brain that this new way of being is not just possible but real.

6. Practice Consistency

Repetition is key. Just as it takes time to master a new skill, programming your mind requires consistent effort. The more you align your thoughts, beliefs, and actions with your goals, the more automatic this process will become.

Why It Matters

Your RAS is like the software running behind the scenes of your brain. By reprogramming it to support your goals, you ensure that your thoughts, habits, and decisions are aligned with the life you want to create.

Remember, your subconscious mind doesn't distinguish between what's real and imagined—it only believes what you repeatedly tell it.

Make sure your words, actions, and beliefs work in harmony, and you'll discover that your goals, dreams, and desires are well within reach.

The Way Your Brain and Subconscious Mind Work Together

Imagine your brain as a highly advanced computer and your subconscious mind as the operating system running in the background. Your brain is the powerhouse—the hardware—containing all the wiring, processing power, connections, and memory needed to help you function at your best. The subconscious mind, on the other hand, acts as the invisible force, influencing how your brain and body work together to accomplish the goals you set.

These two elements—your brain and subconscious mind—are intimately connected. Together, they are essential to your transformation into the person you want to be and achieving the dreams you've set for yourself.

The Brain: The Processor of Your Actions

Your brain is a marvel of complexity, with billions of neurons facilitating communication between your body and your nervous system. These neurons are constantly transmitting signals that guide your actions, thoughts, and behaviors. What's fascinating is that much of this happens at an unconscious level.

For example, think about the automatic processes that keep you alive: breathing, digestion, heartbeat, blinking, and even your body's internal temperature regulation. None of these functions require conscious effort. Your body simply does them—without you needing to think about it.

This unconscious functionality is a reflection of how your brain and subconscious mind work together to manage your physical state.

And just as your body effortlessly performs these automatic tasks, so too can your brain and subconscious mind be conditioned to act in alignment with your goals—without constant conscious effort.

The Subconscious Mind: The Influencer of Your Actions

While your brain processes and stores information, your subconscious mind holds the keys to your behaviors, habits, and deep-rooted beliefs. It's like the software driving the hardware of your brain. Just as your operating system manages background tasks on a computer, your subconscious mind influences your actions, emotions, and responses to the world around you.

The goal is to align your subconscious mind with the actions and results you desire. When you train your subconscious mind to support your goals, the behaviors necessary to achieve them become automatic and habitual. This is how you begin to "program" your brain and subconscious mind for success.

The Cognitive Load: Lightening the Mental Burden

So why is understanding how your brain and subconscious mind work together so important? Because it directly affects your cognitive load—the mental energy required to perform tasks and make decisions. Just like a cluttered room makes it hard to think or move freely, a cluttered mind makes it difficult to focus on what's most important.

By training your brain and subconscious to automatically handle certain tasks and behaviors, you free up mental space to focus on bigger, more impactful things. This is why habits are so crucial. The more you can rewire your brain to handle tasks without conscious effort, the more mental energy you can reserve for your goals.

Think of it like decluttering your mind to make room for the most important furniture, your dreams, your goals, your vision for the future. But this won't happen overnight.

Just as learning a new skill takes time, reprogramming your mind to work in your favor requires consistent practice.

Creating New Habits: The Path to Automatic Success

To transform your life, you need to create new thought patterns and behaviors that support your goals. This takes time, effort, and repetition.

Start by visualizing yourself achieving your dreams. See the people, places, and experiences you want to manifest as if they are already part of your reality. Emotionally connect with these visions daily, and with time, your brain will begin to accept these images as truths. Eventually, these new beliefs and behaviors will become automatic and habitual.

Identifying Unconscious Roadblocks

Before diving into the process of reprogramming your brain and subconscious mind, it's essential to take stock of the habits and beliefs that are currently running in the background. These unconscious patterns may be the very things that are preventing you from reaching your potential.

Identifying these roadblocks is crucial to moving forward. They are the limiting beliefs or destructive behaviors that keep you from progressing. Once you understand what's holding you back, you can begin to clear the path toward success.

Understanding the Roadblocks

Why is it so important to uncover these unconscious roadblocks? Because they may be directly affecting how you approach your goals. They might be the reason you procrastinate, doubt yourself, or avoid taking risks. By understanding these mental blocks, you gain the power to change them.

It's only when you recognize these obstacles that you can start to consciously work around them, replacing limiting beliefs with empowering ones that align with your desires. Understanding the barriers to success allows you to navigate the journey toward achieving your dreams more effectively.

In Conclusion

Your brain and subconscious mind are incredibly powerful allies in your quest for success. By understanding how they work together, you can begin to train them to align with your goals and dreams. With practice, consistency, and awareness, you can rewire your mind to automatically work toward the life you desire.

So, take the time to declutter your mind, challenge your limiting beliefs, and create new habits that support your success. As you do, you'll begin to experience more clarity, less resistance, and a stronger sense of alignment between where you are now and where you want to be. The transformation you seek begins within.

Transforming Your Belief System

Your belief system is like the operating system of your life. It runs in the background of your subconscious mind, guiding every action you take, every decision you make, and even the thoughts you think—whether you're aware of it or not.

Just as an operating system controls a computer's functions, your belief system governs how you navigate life, impacting everything from your relationships to your career, and ultimately your success.

Understanding the beliefs that may be standing in the way of your goals is the first step toward transforming them. Because if you don't address these limiting beliefs, they'll continue to control your actions in a way that prevents you from achieving your full potential.

The Power of Self-Belief

If you constantly tell yourself that you're not good enough or that you're incapable of achieving your goals, then your actions will reflect those beliefs. Doubt creeps in, and before you know it, you start to question why you should even bother trying, assuming failure is inevitable.

This mindset can create a destructive cycle: **fear of failure** paralyzes you, making it harder to push forward. The truth is, if you believe you can't succeed, you're far less likely to put in the effort required to achieve your dreams. You may end up giving up before you even get started.

But here's the thing: **challenges and failures are not signs of defeat—they are opportunities for growth and learning.** You only fail when you give up. The people who succeed are the ones who embrace challenges, knowing that every setback is part of the journey to greater success.

The Danger of Negative Beliefs

If you're trapped in a cycle of negative self-talk, your self-esteem takes a hit.

Constantly believing that you aren't good enough or that you can't achieve your goals gradually chips away at your confidence and mental well-being. Over time, these beliefs may lead to feelings of inadequacy, anxiety, and depression. The more you dwell on them, the stronger they become, creating a vicious cycle that can last a lifetime.

But here's the good news: you can break this cycle. The first step is awareness. You have to be honest with yourself and recognize when negative beliefs are sabotaging your progress. **Awareness is the gateway to change.**

The Path to Transforming Your Belief System

1. Cultivate Self-Awareness

Start by paying attention to your thoughts and feelings. Notice when you catch yourself thinking negatively. Do you find yourself saying things like, "I'm not good enough" or "I'll never be able to do this"? When you do, pause and challenge those thoughts. Ask yourself: **Are these thoughts true? Are they serving me?** If the answer is no, consciously let go of them and replace them with empowering beliefs that align with your goals and aspirations.

2. Educate Yourself

Sometimes, our beliefs are rooted in a lack of knowledge or outdated information. By educating yourself, you can replace limiting beliefs with facts, and build a belief system that supports your personal growth. Knowledge helps dispel fears and opens your mind to possibilities that you may not have considered before.

3. Surround Yourself with Positivity

The people and environment around you have a huge influence on your beliefs. If you're surrounded by negativity or people who don't support your goals, it's easy to adopt limiting beliefs as your own. To counteract this, seek out positive influences—people who uplift and encourage you, who inspire you to believe in yourself. A supportive environment can make all the difference in your ability to maintain a positive belief system.

4. Take Care of Yourself

Self-care isn't just about pampering yourself—it's about taking care of your physical, emotional, and mental well-being. Regular exercise, a balanced diet, and adequate sleep can help reduce stress and improve your overall health.

When you feel good physically, your mental clarity improves, making it easier to maintain a positive outlook and a belief in your ability to achieve your goals.

5. Practice Self-Compassion

It's important to be kind to yourself. Everyone makes mistakes and faces challenges—that's part of being human. Instead of criticizing yourself when things don't go according to plan, treat yourself with the same compassion and understanding you would offer to a friend. Recognize that growth is a process, and every mistake is a valuable lesson on the way to success.

Moving Forward with a New Belief System

Transforming your belief system takes time and consistent effort. It's not about changing who you are at your core; it's about removing the limiting beliefs that are standing in the way of your true potential. Once you replace these outdated, negative beliefs with ones that support your vision, you'll find that achieving your goals becomes much easier.

Remember, your beliefs shape your reality. If you believe that success is possible, and if you're willing to work toward it with determination and faith in yourself, there's no limit to what you can achieve. So, take the time to reflect, reprogram your mind, and create a belief system that empowers you to become the person you were always meant to be.

Maximizing Your Expectations: Creating the Future You Desire

When it comes to creating the future you've always envisioned, it's easy to become fixated on your expectations. But here's the catch: holding on too tightly to these expectations can often leave you feeling unfocused, disconnected from the present moment, and stuck in the pursuit of your goals.

In fact, if you find yourself caught up in the future too much, it can hinder your ability to actually move forward and create the life you desire.

So, what's the solution? **Live in the present moment.** While it's crucial to have clear goals and a vision for your future, it's just as important to stay grounded in the present. This balance—between planning for tomorrow and fully experiencing today—will help you appreciate what you have, while still staying focused on what you're working toward. After all, no one else is going to be more invested in your life than you are.

Living in the present allows you to save yourself the unnecessary stress and worry that come from focusing on the uncertainties of life. By staying grounded in the here and now, you can manage challenges as they arise without being overwhelmed by what's yet to come.

This focus on the present moment frees your mind to take action without the weight of the future holding you back.

The Power of Expectations in Shaping Reality

There's a powerful truth that often goes overlooked: **we tend to get from life what we expect to get.** Expectations send a clear signal to your subconscious mind about what is possible, and more importantly, what is inevitable. When you expect something to happen, your subconscious mind perceives it as a reality. As a result, it aligns your actions, thoughts, and behaviors with that expectation, making it more likely to come true.

Expectations aren't just wishful thinking—they are vital, dynamic forces that shape our reality. One of the key steps in turning your dreams into tangible results is not only reconditioning your beliefs and behaviors but also **shifting your expectations**. By changing your expectations, you alter the way your mind and body respond to opportunities, challenges, and even setbacks.

Why is this crucial? Because **your expectations** play an enormous role in shaping your thoughts and actions, and it's these thoughts and actions that ultimately create your reality. The more you expect success and growth, the more aligned your subconscious mind will become with that outcome, creating a self-fulfilling prophecy of achievement.

Competing with Daily Life: Training Your Mind for Success

The reality we experience is created moment by moment, thought by thought, and action by action. If you want to transform your life, you must consciously and consistently program your brain to focus on the future you want—while still engaging in the present moment.

Picture this: every time you visualize yourself achieving your goals and feel the emotions that come with that success, you're essentially training your brain.

By moving your body as though you're already living your desired life, you send signals to your subconscious mind that your future reality is already in motion. Over time, this practice helps solidify the new beliefs and behaviors that will lead you to your goals.

Research shows that our brains are hard-wired to create mental images of the world we believe is possible. And with each repetition, whether real or imagined, we reinforce these mental images, strengthening the synaptic connections that will eventually make those images our new reality. The more you immerse yourself in these visualizations and embody your desired future, the quicker your brain will rewire itself to make it happen.

Rewriting Your Reality Code: Shifting Your Thought Patterns

Creating the life you want isn't just about thinking differently, it's about **acting** differently and making those actions habitual.

The more you practice new thought patterns and behaviors, the faster your brain will integrate them into your long-term memory, enabling you to act without thinking.

As you work to change your mindset, your brain begins to shift from a default mode of thinking to an active mode. In this state, your subconscious mind will no longer have to consciously direct your thoughts—you will naturally think and act in alignment with your goals. The key to this transformation is repetition. The more you practice new ways of thinking and behaving, the more automatic these actions will become.

This is why your mornings are crucial. The first few minutes of your day set the tone for everything that follows. If you begin each morning with clear, positive intentions—visualizing success and embodying the person you wish to become—you send a powerful message to your brain that you are committed to your future.

The Importance of Changing Your State

To anchor your new reality, it's essential to **master your mental state**. When you consistently train your brain and subconscious mind to remain in a positive, empowered state, your body and mind begin to naturally produce the chemical compounds associated with that state. As a result, you stay in that positive state more often, reinforcing the mindset that supports your goals.

Why is this so important? Because the ultimate goal is to condition your brain to remain in this positive, empowered state as you move forward. This mindset becomes your foundation—the lens through which you view the world, take action and respond to challenges. With every step, your brain will produce the thoughts and emotions that align with your desired reality.

Conclusion: Maximizing Your Expectations for Success

Maximizing your expectations isn't about ignoring the challenges that arise or pretending that everything is always perfect. Instead, it's about understanding the incredible power of your mind to shape your reality. By conditioning your brain, adjusting your expectations, and living with intention, you align your subconscious mind with the success you seek.

Remember, your future doesn't happen by accident. It's created by the actions you take today, the thoughts you think, and the expectations you hold. So, train your mind to focus on what's possible, and trust that every step you take will bring you closer to the life you were meant to live.

Anchoring Your Mental State: The Power of Creating Positive Change

One of the most profound ways to steer your life toward success and fulfillment is by **anchoring** yourself to a positive mental and emotional state. This anchoring process serves as a powerful tool to guide your thoughts, actions, and behaviors in a more productive, goal-oriented direction. But how does one achieve this transformation?

Let's explore the steps required to anchor your mental state and set the foundation for success.

Step 1: Envisioning Your Desired Future

The first step toward anchoring yourself in a positive mental state is to **visualize** yourself as the person you aspire to be, living the life you've always dreamed of. This step is essential because it helps establish a clear and vivid mental picture of your future, which will act as the blueprint for your subconscious mind.

Dive deep into the sensory details of this visualization—**see, hear, and feel** everything as if it is happening in real-time. What does your ideal life look like?

What are the emotions you're experiencing in that moment? The more detailed and emotionally charged your visualization, the stronger the neurological connection your brain will form.

The goal is to reach a peak emotional and mental state—one where you're fully immersed in this vision. Once you've achieved this heightened state, the next crucial step is to create an **anchor** that will allow you to access this state at will.

Step 2: Creating Your Anchor

You might be wondering, what exactly is an anchor? Simply put, an anchor is a physical or mental trigger that links a specific experience or emotional state to a particular stimulus. This stimulus can be anything—a hand gesture, a facial expression, or even a specific word or phrase. The key is that it's something that, when activated, will **automatically return you** to that peak mental and emotional state you experienced during your visualization.

For instance, perhaps you associate a deep sense of confidence and calmness with a simple gesture, like touching your fingers together. The more you practice this anchor while in your peak emotional state, the stronger the connection between the anchor and the positive mental state becomes. It's like training a muscle—the more you exercise it, the stronger it gets.

Step 3: Repetition and Conditioning

The next critical aspect of anchoring your mental state is repetition. The more you consciously and consistently use your anchor to return to your desired mental and emotional state, the quicker it will become automatic. This process relies on the brain's incredible ability to **learn through association**.

Our brains are designed to remember and store experiences by associating new information with existing patterns.

This is the principle behind **neuroplasticity**, the brain's ability to reorganize and form new neural connections throughout our lives. The more frequently you activate your anchor and connect it to positive emotions, the stronger the neuro-association becomes. Eventually, it will be ingrained in your subconscious, and your brain will automatically trigger the desired mental state whenever you need it.

The Science Behind Learning: Episodic vs. Semantic Memory

To fully understand how anchoring works, it's helpful to dive into how our brains store and retrieve memories. Our brain processes our experiences through two types of memory: **episodic** and **semantic**.

Episodic memory is the personal, emotionally charged memory of specific events—these memories are tied to particular times and places. For example, remembering a trip to Paris: the taste of the croissant, the sound of the French language, the feelings of joy and wonder. These sensory details are stored in episodic memory and are often more deeply ingrained because they are attached to strong emotions.

In contrast, **semantic memory** is based on knowledge, facts, and concepts that we learn through observation or study. It doesn't rely on personal experiences or emotions but is the kind of memory we tap into when recalling data or learned skills.

When you create strong, positive emotional connections to your visualizations and anchors, you are essentially encoding these experiences both **episodically and semantically**. The emotional charge you attach to these memories enhances their retention, ensuring that they stay with you long after the experience has passed.

The Role of Neuroplasticity: Rewiring Your Brain for Success

Now, let's discuss the core process that enables all of this transformation: **neuroplasticity**. Neuroplasticity refers to the brain's ability to reorganize itself by forming new neural connections throughout life.

This ability is what allows you to **learn new behaviors, adapt to change, and create lasting transformation**.

Every time you practice your mental anchoring, you are performing an action or thought that physically rewires your brain. Neuroplasticity makes it possible for you to develop new habits and thought patterns by repeatedly activating the neural circuits associated with those behaviors. As the neuroscientist Donald Hebb famously said, "Neurons that fire together, wire together."

By continuously focusing on your goals, visualizing your success, and anchoring yourself to positive emotions, your brain will start to form new synaptic connections that reinforce your desired outcomes. The more you engage in this process, the stronger these neural pathways become, leading to a transformation in how you see the world and yourself.

Conclusion: Rewiring Your Brain for Success

Anchoring your mental state is more than just a technique, it's a **profound shift in how you approach your life and goals**. By consistently visualizing your desired future, creating emotional connections to those visions, and reinforcing them with anchors, you gradually rewire your brain to align with the success you seek.

Through neuroplasticity, you have the power to create new thought patterns and behaviors that become automatic over time.

As your brain forms new neural connections, it becomes increasingly easier to maintain a positive mental state, respond to challenges with resilience, and take the actions necessary to achieve your goals.

This process doesn't happen overnight, but with time, commitment, and consistency, you will reprogram your brain for success. By anchoring yourself to a positive mental state, you'll create a life that reflects the highest version of yourself—the person you've always aspired to be.

The Power of Imagination: Shaping Your Reality

At the heart of creating the life you envision lies a profound tool we all possess: **the power of imagination**. By consciously training and conditioning your brain to think and act in ways that align with your desires, you can shape your reality. The key is to harness your imagination, using pictures and images to craft your future until those mental images become so ingrained in your mind that they turn into automatic, habitual actions.

Why Imagination is Crucial

Why is this process so essential? Simply put, **our brains think and remember in pictures**. This natural ability to process the world in visual terms is a unique skill that, when fully understood, can be leveraged to design the life we want to live. Whether those mental images are drawn from real experiences or imagined scenarios, they have the power to shape the way we perceive ourselves and the world around us.

When you immerse yourself in the imagery of the life you desire, whether real or imagined, your brain begins to treat those images as reality. **The more you condition your subconscious mind to arrange and rearrange these images**, the easier it becomes to trigger your brain and body to re-experience them in real-time.

The brain cannot always differentiate between what is real and what is vividly imagined—what matters is the emotional and cognitive engagement that accompanies the visualization.

Organizing Your Mental Imagery

The key to successfully conditioning your mind is organizing these images into **chronological and systematic order**.

Why is this important? Because the more you structure the experiences you wish to manifest in your mind, the easier it becomes to recall them at will. This order enables your brain to process and file them away in a way that mimics the process of remembering real-life experiences, ensuring that they become a natural part of your mental and emotional landscape.

When your brain recognizes these organized images as part of its natural system for organizing memory, it allows you to think and act from these images with ease. The result is a seamless integration of your desired reality into your thoughts, behaviors, and actions.

Exercise in Imagination: A Simple Proof

Let's put this idea into practice with a simple exercise. Close your eyes for a moment and imagine your living room. Picture every item in the room—the furniture, decorations, and layout. Now, think about the exact placement of each item. You should be able to visualize every detail with clarity and precision. This is because your brain has already categorized and stored these images within your memory system.

The reason you can recall these images so effortlessly is that your brain has already organized them into a mental filing system. Your mind doesn't need to consciously search for the objects; instead, it relies on these images, which have become part of your automatic mental framework.

This exercise proves a crucial point: **the brain naturally creates and organizes images of the world around us**, and it uses these images to help us navigate our lives. So, why not apply the same principle to the life you want to create?

The Key to Creating Your Desired Reality

The process of creating your desired reality works in much the same way. To manifest the life you dream of, you must consciously organize the pictures and images of your ideal experiences—people, places, and events—into a structured, chronological order. Over time, these mental images will become so ingrained that your brain will treat them just like the memories of things that already exist in your life.

This is where the power of imagination takes root. **As your mind organizes and prioritizes these mental images,** they start to become part of your everyday thinking, influencing how you see yourself and the world around you. The more vivid and clear these images are, the more your brain will accept them as reality, shaping your actions and behaviors to match the life you wish to live.

Living from the Inside Out

Remember, we live in a world shaped by the thoughts and images in our minds—not just by the external reality around us. By engaging with your desired experiences through imagination, you begin to **live from the inside out**. The more frequently you practice this, the easier it will be to **experience those desired realities in real-time**, whether or not they've physically manifested yet.

When you immerse yourself in the thoughts, emotions, and actions of the life you want, your brain starts to adapt to those patterns. Even if these experiences are imagined, your brain does not distinguish between what is real and what is vividly imagined. It simply responds to the neural pathways that have been activated, and the more often those pathways are activated, the stronger they become.

The Neuroscience of Repetition: Creating Automatic Habits

This process of repetition leads to something powerful: the development of **automatic habits**. As your brain continuously engages with these imagined scenarios, neural connections are formed, strengthened, and reinforced. These connections make the thoughts and behaviors associated with your desired life more automatic, and more ingrained.

Neuroscientists call this **neuroplasticity**—the brain's ability to rewire itself through repetition. Every time you imagine yourself living the life you want, your brain builds new neural networks that support those visions. Eventually, these networks become so strong that your actions, decisions, and behaviors begin to reflect the images you've created in your mind, allowing you to live out your desired reality more effortlessly.

Conclusion: Harnessing the Power of Your Imagination

In essence, the power of imagination lies in your ability to shape your mind and body through the mental images you choose to focus on. By organizing those images, engaging with them emotionally, and repeating them regularly, you can **condition your brain to create the reality you desire**.

The clearer and more detailed your mental pictures, the more your brain will accept them as part of your lived experience, shaping how you think, act, and ultimately live. As you continue to practice this, your desired reality will naturally unfold, not as something distant or unattainable, but as something that is already woven into the fabric of your daily life.

Exercise in Relaxation: A Gateway to Clarity and Focus

First and foremost, let me take a moment to congratulate you for making it this far in the book. The fact that you've committed yourself to this journey is something to be proud of.

But I want to encourage you to keep going because we're just getting started. Now, though, let's pause for a moment and take a step back to process everything you've learned so far.

This next exercise is all about **relaxation**, a simple yet powerful tool that will not only help you unwind but also enhance your focus and clarity. Why? Because absorbing new information, especially the valuable insights we've explored up until now, can be mentally taxing. Our brains work hard to process and integrate knowledge, and sometimes the best thing we can do is give it the space it needs to rest and rejuvenate.

So, let's take a break together. Take a deep breath and simply allow yourself to **relax**.

Preparing for the Relaxation Process

Find a quiet space where you can be alone for a few minutes. This could be anywhere—your bedroom, a cozy corner, or even a spot outdoors where you feel comfortable and undisturbed. Once you're settled, close your eyes, and allow the noise of the world around you to fade into the background. At this moment, there's nothing to worry about, no tasks, no obligations. Simply be present.

Now, let's begin by focusing on your breath. Take a slow, deliberate breath through your nose. As the cool air enters your nostrils, **feel it traveling down your throat**, slowly filling your lungs. With each breath, you're drawing in life-giving oxygen. Expand your diaphragm as you inhale, filling your lungs as fully as possible. Let the air spread throughout your chest, filling your body with fresh energy.

Hold that breath for a moment—just a few seconds, feeling the oxygen circulate, nourishing every cell in your body. Notice how this small moment of stillness creates a feeling of **presence**—a sensation that you are here, now, in this very moment.

Releasing Tension and Embracing Calm

When you're ready, exhale gently through your mouth. As you do, imagine releasing not only the air from your lungs but also any tension or stress that you may be holding onto. With each exhale, let your thoughts slow down and your body relax.

To deepen the relaxation, you can visualize a peaceful scene in your mind—a serene forest, the gentle waves of a quiet beach, or perhaps a sunlit meadow. Picture every detail of this scene as vividly as possible. Alternatively, you can silently repeat the word **"relax"** to yourself, letting its soothing rhythm act like a mantra guiding you into a state of calm.

Focus on the rhythm of your breathing: inhale slowly, exhale gently. Take your time with each breath, feeling the air enter and leave your body. Notice how each cycle of breathing feels more calming than the last.

Deepening Your Relaxation

Continue this cycle of breathing—inhale, hold, exhale—for about ten repetitions. With each breath, you'll begin to notice that your body is releasing tension, and your mind is growing clearer. The more you focus on your breath, the less room there is for distractions or worries. Your thoughts will become sharper, more focused, and more in tune with the present moment.

At some point, you may notice a slight dizziness. This is completely normal. It's simply a response to the increased oxygen circulating in your brain. If you feel lightheaded, just take a moment to pause and allow your body to adjust. Don't rush the process. The goal is to let your body and mind find a rhythm that feels natural and calming.

Transforming Nervous Energy into Productive Energy

This relaxation exercise is far more than just a simple technique for calming your nerves—it's a **tool for transformation**. By focusing on your breath, you're teaching your body to shift from a state of anxious energy into one of productive focus.

Anxiety and tension often arise from the overwhelming feeling that we have too much to do or too much to think about. This exercise helps you regain control by redirecting your energy from a state of stress to one of **calm focus**.

When you take time to center yourself in the present, you shift your mental and emotional state. You train your body and mind to respond to challenges with clarity, rather than fear or overwhelm. As you continue to practice this relaxation technique, you'll find it easier to tap into this state of calm focus whenever you need it—whether you're working through a difficult task, preparing for an important meeting, or simply managing the everyday stresses of life.

The Ongoing Journey of Relaxation

Remember, relaxation is not a one-time experience, it's practice. The more you engage in this exercise, the more you'll deepen your ability to **manage your mental and emotional states**. This will have a profound impact not just on how you approach challenges but also on how you relate to yourself and the world around you.

By learning to relax and breathe deeply, you're not just giving your mind a break; you're cultivating a **skill that empowers you** to maintain focus, clarity, and peace in any situation.

Take a moment to congratulate yourself for taking this step. By learning to relax and breathe, you've taken the first steps toward mastering your mental and emotional wellbeing. As we continue, you'll see how these simple practices will build upon each other, allowing you to create the life you desire—one step, one breath at a time.

In Chapter 6, you'll explore the transformative practice of self-hypnosis to unlock your potential and program your mind for success. This chapter teaches you how to access deeper mental states, break free from limitations, and reinforce beliefs that drive greatness.

Here's what you'll learn:

- **What Self-Hypnosis Is and Isn't:** Understand the science and myths of hypnosis and why it's a powerful tool for self-improvement.

- **Guiding Yourself into Hypnosis:** Learn step-by-step techniques to relax your mind and body and enter a hypnotic state.

- **Creating Powerful Hypnotic Suggestions:** Discover how to craft affirmations and commands that align with your goals and subconscious programming.

- **Overcoming Mental Blocks:** Use self-hypnosis to eliminate negative thought patterns, self-doubt, and limiting beliefs.

- **Reinforcing Positive Habits:** Program your mind to stay focused, motivated, and aligned with your vision.

- **Daily Integration:** Learn best practices for incorporating self-hypnosis into your routine for consistent growth and transformation.

By the end of this chapter, you'll have practical tools to reprogram your mind, harness your subconscious, and unlock a level of greatness you never thought possible.

HOW TO HYPNOTIZE YOURSELF FOR GREATNESS

"The only limit to our realization of tomorrow is our doubts of today."

— *Franklin D. Roosevelt*

The path to achieving greatness is not defined by a singular event, but by an underlying belief that success is not just possible—it is inevitable. This powerful belief, which some might call confidence or faith, is the cornerstone of success. **Successful people believe in their success before they even achieve it.** They expect to win, even when the outcome is uncertain. This unwavering conviction is what drives their actions, creating momentum and determination to keep pushing forward, regardless of external circumstances. Before you can turn your dreams into reality, you must first cultivate this belief within yourself, and this is where the practice of self-hypnosis comes into play.

The Power of Self-Hypnosis

Before you dismiss hypnosis as something mystical or reserved for deep trance states, let's define it more simply: **hypnosis is a natural and automatic state of focused attention**. We all experience it regularly—whether it's when you get lost in a book, zone out while driving, or lose track of time during a creative project. These moments of deep focus are hypnotic states, and they are powerful tools for influencing your subconscious mind.

Why is this important? Because **all hypnosis is self-hypnosis.** The ability to consciously enter and direct these states is what gives you the power to reprogram your mind for success.

Hypnosis is simply the gateway to reprogramming your brain to automatically align your thoughts, behaviors, and actions with your goals and aspirations.

The Subconscious: Your Mind's Powerhouse

To truly harness the power of your mind, you must understand the relationship between the conscious and subconscious parts of your brain. The conscious mind is what you're aware of in the present moment—the thoughts, decisions, and observations you actively engage with. But **the subconscious mind** is far more powerful, influencing roughly **95% of your actions and behaviors.**

This is why **you must bypass the conscious mind** and speak directly to the subconscious if you want to program your brain to work in your favor. Your subconscious is where your automatic behaviors and habitual thoughts reside. It operates based on deep-seated beliefs, memories, and patterns you've built over time—often without your conscious awareness.

Programming Your Brain with Certainty

To truly program your brain for success, you must speak to the subconscious mind in a language it understands: **certainty**. The more you use statements of certainty, the more your subconscious begins to align with them. This is why affirmations, or positive self-talk can be so effective. But it's not just about speaking affirmations, you must **feel the truth of those words in your body**.

When you declare something with conviction, your subconscious mind doesn't question it. It simply accepts it as truth and starts forming behaviors to make it a reality.

For example, when you tell yourself, "I am confident and capable," your brain starts to look for ways to prove that you are. This consistency of self-assurance primes your brain to take actions that align with your goals.

You are, in essence, creating a mental framework that functions like **embedded commands**, programming your brain to act and think in alignment with your desires.

The more you reinforce this belief, the more it becomes ingrained in your neural pathways, leading to automatic, habitual behaviors that move you toward success.

Priming Your Brain for Success

Before you can fully control your thoughts, it's important to understand the concept of **priming. Priming is the process of preparing your brain to respond to certain stimuli** by triggering thoughts and behaviors that are already stored within your mind. Every decision, every action, is preceded by a thought—a preparatory mental cue that often operates below the surface of your awareness.

Priming works by **activating thoughts that are already linked in your mind**. For instance, when you think of the word "success," your brain automatically activates related words and ideas—such as "achievement," "growth," "confidence," or "leadership." These associations trigger a cascade of related thoughts and behaviors, making it easier for your mind to follow through with actions aligned with those concepts.

The Science Behind Priming

Priming is not just a mental trick; it is rooted in the **neuroplasticity of the brain**. The more frequently you associate certain words or experiences with specific feelings or behaviors, the stronger the neural connections become.

This means that by carefully choosing the words you use—both in your inner dialogue and when speaking to others—you can shape your reality.

For example, imagine starting your day by telling yourself, "I am focused, capable, and unstoppable." The words "focused," "capable," and "unstoppable" prime your brain to look for evidence that supports these beliefs.

The more you say these words, the more your brain is primed to seek out situations and behaviors that match them. Over time, these words will become an automatic part of your vocabulary, shaping not only your thoughts but also your actions.

Programming Your Mind for Action

As you continue priming your brain with the right words and thoughts, it becomes easier to **act in alignment with your goals**. These words create neural pathways that make it more natural for you to think and behave in ways that serve your desires. The more you prime yourself with thoughts of success, growth, and confidence, the more you train your mind to automatically engage in behaviors that lead to these outcomes.

The truth is, achieving greatness begins with your **belief in your own success**—before you have any evidence to prove it. This belief is not just a wish; it's a force that will drive you to act, learn, and grow. As you continue to program your mind through self-hypnosis, certainty, and priming, you'll find that your thoughts and behaviors naturally align with your goals, and success will become not just a possibility, but an inevitability.

By mastering the art of self-hypnosis and priming your brain for success, you are unlocking a deeper power within yourself.

You are not waiting for success to come to you—you are **creating it from the inside out**, cultivating a mindset that propels you forward even when the path is uncertain. The first step to greatness is believing in your success, and with the power of your mind, you can achieve anything you set your sights on.

Using Certainty to Prime Your Subconscious

To create lasting success, you must first master the art of priming your subconscious mind. One of the most powerful tools at your disposal is the use of **statements of certainty**. These are simple, affirmative statements that reinforce the belief that your goals, dreams, and desires are already on their way to becoming reality.

Start by reflecting on your goals and imagining how success is already unfolding. As you do, consider using statements like these:

- "You've already taken significant steps toward your goals, haven't you?"

- "As soon as you set your goals, didn't you notice things started moving faster?"

- "Think of how much you've learned about yourself throughout this journey."

- "Isn't it worth facing every challenge that comes your way to achieve your dreams?"

These statements do more than just acknowledge your progress—they **affirm to your brain that success is inevitable**. Even when the results are not immediately visible, they create a mental framework where forward movement becomes a natural, automatic process. You are not just hoping for success but actively *expecting* it. This expectation helps establish a **positive mental pattern** that pushes you to continue, even when obstacles arise.

As you consistently use these statements of certainty, you will begin to notice a change in how you think and feel. Each repetition of these affirmations triggers related thoughts that further bolster your belief in your eventual success.

This forms a **cycle of positive reinforcement**, encouraging you to take the necessary actions toward your dreams.

The Power of Words and Thoughts

The words we speak and think have a profound impact on our lives. They do more than simply communicate information; they shape our perceptions, guide our actions, and influence our outcomes. This is the core principle behind **semantic priming**, a psychological phenomenon where one word or idea activates a cascade of related concepts in your mind.

For example, when you say the word "success," your mind might automatically trigger thoughts of **achievement, growth, confidence**, and **empowerment**. Each of these words, in turn, activates a web of thoughts that shape how you feel and behave in response to your goals. This is the power of language in action.

By focusing on words associated with **success, growth**, and **achievement**, you prime your brain to recognize and seize opportunities that align with these concepts. The more you practice this, the more natural and automatic these positive thoughts and behaviors become. Over time, you will find yourself gravitating toward the very outcomes you desire, because your brain is now wired to seek them out.

Controlling Your Thoughts: The Key to Mastery

Every moment of your life is shaped by the thoughts that precede it. These thoughts are the internal triggers that prompt your actions, decisions, and behaviors. The key to mastering your life and your reality lies in learning to control these thoughts, especially the **thoughts that reinforce your goals and ambitions**.

Through the process of priming, you can consciously choose which thoughts to reinforce, ensuring that they serve your highest potential. By using statements of certainty, you essentially "program" your mind to believe in your success before it's fully realized. This belief becomes the foundation upon which your actions are built, and it propels you toward your goals.

But there's a crucial element to this process: **awareness**. To truly harness the power of priming, you must first become aware of how your mind operates. Once you understand how your thoughts influence your behavior, you can begin to make conscious choices about which thoughts to entertain and which to let go.

Priming for Success: A Continuous Process

To prime your subconscious mind for greatness, you need to consistently feed it with the right words, thoughts, and affirmations. Start by using statements of certainty to reinforce your belief in your own success. These statements should reflect not only your aspirations but also your confidence that they are already unfolding.

Prime your brain by choosing words that align with your goals—words like **success, growth, empowerment,** and **achievement**. The more you use these words, the more they will activate the corresponding thoughts and behaviors that drive you toward your dreams.

But priming alone is not enough. To truly make these changes permanent, you must **take consistent action**. Your mind will work in harmony with your actions, guiding you toward the opportunities and decisions that lead to your success. With every step you take, the neural connections that support your goals grow stronger, and your success becomes not only a possibility but a certainty.

The Inevitable Success

When you program your mind to believe in your success, **success becomes inevitable**.

The certainty with which you approach your goals sets the stage for your mind and body to align with those goals, no matter the challenges you face.

Remember: Your thoughts are powerful. By harnessing the power of certainty, priming, and consistent action, you can rewire your brain for success. **Success is not just something you achieve—it's something you expect, plan for, and create every day.**

In the end, it is the combination of belief, language, and action that unlocks your greatest potential. When your subconscious mind is fully aligned with your goals, your reality will shift to reflect the greatness you've always known was possible.

In Chapter 7, you'll focus on the importance of revisiting and reaffirming your intentions as you progress toward your vision. This chapter teaches you how to realign with your purpose, reinforce your goals, and maintain clarity on your journey.

Here's what you'll learn:

- **The Power of Intention:** Understand why restating your intentions keeps your goals top of mind and strengthens your commitment.

- **Daily Intention Practices:** Learn practical methods to reaffirm your intentions every day, keeping you focused and motivated.

- **Staying Aligned with Your Vision:** Discover how to evaluate your progress and ensure your actions remain consistent with your core purpose.

- **Adjusting Your Intentions:** Explore how to adapt and refine your intentions as you grow and circumstances evolve.

- **Using Intentions to Overcome Challenges:** Learn how restating your intentions can help you stay grounded and resilient during setbacks.

- **Integrating Intentions into Your Identity:** Understand how to make your intentions a natural part of who you are and how you show up in the world.

By the end of this chapter, you'll have a deeper understanding of how to consistently realign with your purpose, refine your goals, and stay connected to the life you're creating. Restating your intentions becomes a powerful habit that ensures you remain intentional and inspired every step of the way.

RESTATE YOUR INTENTIONS

"Clarity in your intentions is the compass that guides you toward your desired destination. When you restate your intentions with conviction, you recalibrate your focus and fuel your commitment to success."

— *Unknown*

Now that you've reached this stage in your journey, it's time to restate your intentions. Why? Because while it's one thing to know who you are and what you want to create in your life, it's another thing entirely to turn that knowledge into action and make it a reality. Don't you agree?

Everything begins with your **intentions**. Why? Because your intention is what sets everything in motion. The clearer you are about what you intend to create, the clearer you understand your **"Why"**— the underlying reason for why you want to pursue this path. This "Why" is the engine that drives your actions, shaping your choices and decisions along the way. As the philosopher Friedrich Nietzsche famously said, *"He who has a why to live for can bear almost any how."*

Understanding your "Why" makes it infinitely easier to figure out the "How"—the strategies, the plans, and the deliberate actions you'll need to implement to transform your goals, dreams, and desires into tangible results.

Focus on What You Want, Not What You Don't Want

The core objective of everything we've covered so far is to help you focus on what you want, not on what you don't want.

Why is this important? Because the moment you shift your mindset to focus solely on the things you want, rather than dwelling on the things you fear or wish to avoid, you begin to create a profound impact on your ability to achieve those goals.

Here's why: We live in a world that is largely shaped by our own minds. The pictures and images we hold in our heads—whether real or imagined—are what give rise to our reality. Our beliefs, particularly those about what is possible, are what manifest our reality.

Research shows that wherever your attention goes, your energy flows. The energy you direct toward something will shape your reality and experiences. So, the more you focus on what you truly want, the more your brain will seek out opportunities that align with those desires. Opportunities, connections, and experiences that resonate with your intentions will begin to appear. Why? Because you always receive back in life what you *feel* you already have. This is the essence of manifestation—your intentions become the **blueprint** for your reality.

The Power of Clarity and Consistent Action

Restating your intentions goes beyond just identifying what you want to create or experience. It involves deeply connecting with your goals, dreams, and desires—and understanding the **motivation** behind them. It's about recognizing the doubts, fears, or limiting beliefs standing in your way and still moving forward, despite them.

But how do you know if your intentions are truly aligned with your authentic self? This is why I guided you through the storytelling and story analysis process at the beginning of this book.

Why? Because before you can create the life you envision, it must resonate with who you truly are at your core. Your authentic self—your values, principles, and aspirations—must be in alignment with your goals.

This alignment makes your journey easier and more fulfilling, as you are inherently motivated by something that is in harmony with your deepest identity.

Ask Yourself: Does This Align With Who I Am?

As you reflect on restating your intentions, ask yourself these critical questions:

- Is this what I truly want to create and experience in my life?
- Does it align with who I believe I am at my core?

If you answer "Yes" to both, congratulations—you are well on your way to creating the life you've always desired. However, if you answer "No" to either question, it may be time to revisit your story. Return to the beginning of this book and re-engage in the **storytelling and story analysis exercise**. Why? Because understanding who you truly are at your core is foundational. If you skipped this process, you might still be unclear on your true purpose or unsure of your next step.

Write It Down: Cement Your Intentions

Now, I want you to take a sheet of paper and write down your **revised intentions**. Reflect on the person you've declared yourself to be and the vision you have set for your life. Why is this important?

Because to **be, have,** and **do** whatever you've set your mind to, you must first become the person you need to be. Only then can you attract the things you want and experience the life you envision—provided you continue taking **consistent** and **purposeful action.**

Once you've written everything down—your **What, Why,** and **How**—set the paper aside and release your immediate focus from it.

Why? Because **letting go** affirms to your subconscious mind that you are fully committed to achieving this goal, no matter how long it takes. As the great psychologist Emile Coué said, *"If you persuade yourself that you can do a certain thing, provided this thing be possible, you will do it, however difficult it may be."*

Become the Person You Need to Be

The key is not whether you **can** or **cannot** achieve your dreams, but whether you **become** the person capable of making them happen.

So, relax. Trust the process. Don't worry about the how or when—just know that you are on your way to turning your imagination into physical reality. The universe responds to your belief. Believe deeply in your power to create and step confidently into the reality you are meant to live.

This is your journey. Embrace it. Because you're not just dreaming of a new reality, you are actively creating it, one intention at a time.

Trust Your Intuition and Stay in the Moment

In this journey of self-discovery and creation, all I ask of you is to trust your intuition and remain in the moment. **Why?** Because your intuition is always speaking to you—it's just not in a language you're not accustomed to. It communicates through your thoughts, feelings, and subtle nudges, but many of us, have stopped listening to it a long time ago. We've been conditioned to rely on logic, reasoning, and external validation, and we've learned to ignore the quiet voice within us.

But here's the truth: you don't need to plan every event, every move, every choice down to the finest detail. You don't need to analyze, rationalize, or overthink every decision. **All you have to do is trust your intuition.**

Your intuition is the inner compass that guides you toward the right direction. It is constantly nudging you, leading you to the opportunities, people, and experiences that will help you realize your dreams. You don't need to have everything figured out—your heart and gut know the way, even if your conscious mind hasn't yet grasped the full picture. The key is to release fear, worry, and stress, and trust that your intuition will guide you, even when the path ahead seems unclear.

The Observer Effect: Creating Your Reality

Why does intuition play such a vital role? Because it's not just about feeling good or making intuitive decisions, it's about something much deeper: **the Observer Effect.** Research has shown that simply observing or thinking about something can have a profound effect on our reality. Our thoughts, our focus, and our very awareness of what we want to create in our lives have the power to shape the reality we experience. When we focus our attention on our desires, even mentally, we are interacting with and influencing the energy around us.

Our minds have the remarkable ability to **create** reality just by thinking about it, watching it, and observing it. Whether we're visualizing, imagining, or recalling a specific event, the mind does not differentiate between what's real and what's imagined. Both are real experiences of the subconscious. In other words, your mind doesn't just observe the world—it **participates** in, shaping the outcomes based on what you focus on.

However, before you can begin creating the reality you desire, you must first heal the **splits** within your personality, your fragmented self. Why is this crucial? Because if you've experienced trauma—whether from childhood or adulthood—your subconscious mind might have created a division within you. This split occurs when the mind attempts to protect itself and creates different aspects of your personality, often in response to unresolved emotional pain.

Healing the Split in Your Personality

Many of us struggle to pursue our goals, dreams, and desires because there is a part of us that is not aligned with who we *truly* are at our core. This misalignment often stems from these fragmented aspects of our personality. When the conscious mind—the aware, rational self—is not in alignment with the unconscious mind, the deeper, hidden self, we often find ourselves torn.

This is where the true work begins: healing the splits in our personalities. Why is this important? Because research shows that these fractured aspects of the self-holds power. They affect how we think, how we behave, and ultimately how we experience life. A piece of our subconscious mind can control our body and actions, influencing the way we think and react—often without us realizing it. The more fragmented our self, the more our conscious mind loses control over our actions and thoughts, surrendering power to the unconscious mind.

To illustrate, think about someone who suffers from a physical ailment—let's say, a person who experiences paralysis or blindness. In many cases, these physical conditions aren't just the result of external causes; they may stem from an inner conflict within the unconscious mind, which deems the condition useful or necessary for some form of protection or survival.

Similarly, there may be a part of you that says, *"I can achieve my dreams. I can go after what I truly want."* But another part of you, perhaps the one that has suffered from past pain or disappointment, whispers, *"Who are you kidding? This isn't for you."*

This internal conflict, the battle between different aspects of your personality—can hold you back from fully stepping into your potential. The dominant part of you, whether the empowered or the fearful part, will dictate your actions and outcomes.

The Power of Healing and Alignment

The ultimate goal is to heal these splits, to align the fragmented pieces of yourself so that your entire being is working in unison. When your conscious self is in agreement with your subconscious self, there is no internal resistance. You are free to pursue your goals, dreams, and desires without hesitation or fear.

So, I ask you: are you ready to listen to your intuition, to trust it even when the path isn't entirely clear? Are you prepared to heal the fractures within yourself and step into the fullness of who you are meant to be?

Trusting your intuition and healing the splits within your personality is not just about achieving success. They are about aligning with your true self and allowing your authentic power to shape the reality you desire. It is in this space of alignment, where intuition and consciousness meet, that you will create the life you've always dreamed of.

Healing the Fragmented Self

Research has shown that the first step in healing a fragmented self is to **identify** the aspects of your personality that are disconnected or holding you back. Once you can pinpoint these parts of yourself, the process of integration becomes much clearer.

The key is to **recognize** these fragmented pieces, name them, and communicate directly with them to begin the process of reintegration.

Why? Because every fragment of your personality has its own mind, its own voice. These fragmented parts often operate from a place of fear, insecurity, or past trauma, which can limit your potential and keep you from achieving your dreams. To heal the fragmentation, you must identify these aspects and understand their influence over your actions, thoughts, and beliefs.

Let's take a common example. Perhaps you find yourself afraid of being seen or heard. Maybe you're terrified of success or feel like you're not good enough, smart enough, or attractive enough to achieve what others do. There's a part of your personality that harbors these fears, one that doesn't believe in your potential. This part might be the result of past experiences, harsh judgments from others, or even messages you internalized growing up.

Your task is to identify the fragmented parts of yourself and understand their root causes. Where did it come from? What part of you is speaking when you have these doubts? And most importantly, how can you reclaim your power?

Speaking to Your Fragmented Self

The process of speaking to your fragmented self requires curiosity and patience. Begin by asking that part of you: What is stopping me from going after my goals, dreams, and desires? What is holding me back from reaching my full potential?

Pause. Wait for an answer.

At first, the response from your fragmented self may surprise you. It might say something like, "I'm afraid of being seen and heard. I don't feel like I'm attractive enough to be visible or successful. I fear that people will judge me, based on how I look or what I say."

Now, ask: Where did that thought come from?

Perhaps the answer is even more revealing. Your fragmented self might respond, "It came from your father. He always told you that you weren't attractive enough."

This is an important moment. You're uncovering the origin of a belief that has shaped your actions, often without you even realizing it. Keep asking questions—What else? Why else do I believe this?

What other thoughts are fueling this fear? Continue until the fragmented self-reveals the full story.

The goal is to unearth the doubts, fears, and insecurities that have been buried deep within you. Often, these beliefs are not even your own, they are inherited from past experiences, family messages, or societal pressures. They may no longer serve you, but they have been dictating your life for far too long.

Bringing the Fragments Together

Once you've thoroughly explored the fears and doubts holding you back, the next step is to bring these fragmented parts of yourself together. **Ask them to reintegrate**—to align with the person you are becoming, the person you have decided to be.

You may say, *"I acknowledge you. I understand why you feel the way you do. But it's time to unite with the rest of me. It's time to heal and move forward. I need you to help me stand my ground and create the reality I've always wanted."*

This isn't a one-time process, it's a journey. But once these fragmented parts are acknowledged and integrated, you'll notice a shift. You'll start to feel more whole, more aligned with your true self. No longer will those limiting beliefs hold power over you. You will become the person who has the clarity and confidence to pursue your goals, free from the constraints of the past.

Healing the fragmented self is about reclaiming your personal power and integrating all the parts of you that may have been lost or suppressed. It's about coming into alignment with your true essence, uniting all aspects of your personality so that you can step fully into your potential.

As you heal, you will begin to see opportunities open up that you never thought possible. When you trust yourself, every part of yourself—your full potential will emerge, and the reality you desire will start to manifest. The key is to **listen**, **heal**, and **unite**.

Healing the Fragmented Self with the Power of the Superconscious Mind

Research has shown that healing the fragmented self requires an intentional process of self-awareness, integration, and reconnection. The first step is to identify the aspects of your personality that are out of alignment, or that feel disconnected from your true, authentic self. These fragmented parts often stem from past experiences, unresolved emotions, or limiting beliefs that no longer serve you. The journey of healing begins with recognizing these fragments and understanding their impact on your current reality.

Why is this important? Because each fragmented part of you carries a story, often deeply rooted in past trauma or negative conditioning.

These fragmented selves have their own mindset, their own way of thinking, and their own beliefs about who you are and what you can achieve. To heal, you must not only recognize these parts but also actively communicate with them and bring them back into alignment with your higher self. This is where the power of your **superconscious mind** comes into play.

What is the Superconscious Mind?

Gary Flint, a renowned expert in the field of personal transformation, emphasizes the importance of connecting with the **superconscious mind** as a tool for healing and personal growth. The superconscious mind is the higher, expansive part of our consciousness that holds access to our deepest wisdom, inner guidance, and the ability to reshape our beliefs and behaviors. It is a source of creative power, insight, and deep inner knowing.

While the conscious mind is often bogged down by doubts and external influences, the superconscious is a channel to our most authentic and empowered self.

The superconscious mind holds the ability to not only transform our perception of reality but also to heal and reintegrate the fragmented parts of our personality. It can bridge the gap between the conscious mind (which may be overwhelmed by fear or confusion) and the unconscious mind (which holds deeper memories and patterns). When you speak to your fragmented self through the lens of your superconscious, you tap into a wellspring of guidance that knows how to heal, restore, and unify your being.

Speaking to Your Fragmented Self Through the Superconscious Mind

So how do you speak to your fragmented self using the superconscious mind? According to Gary Flint, it all begins with intentional **focus** and **dialogue**. The superconscious mind responds to clarity and intention. It can hear your inner desires, understand your core beliefs, and assist in reshaping the fragments that hold you back.

Step 1: Enter a State of Deep Relaxation

The first step in connecting with your superconscious mind is to quiet the noise of your everyday thoughts. This is achieved through relaxation techniques such as deep breathing, meditation, or guided imagery. When you enter a calm, focused state, you begin to create a pathway for your superconscious mind to communicate with you.

Step 2: Ask the Right Questions

Once you've entered this relaxed state, begin by asking your fragmented self-specific questions that will help uncover the limiting beliefs or patterns holding you back. Ask with the understanding that your superconscious mind has access to deeper insights and can help you uncover the root cause of your fears or doubts. For example:

- *What is stopping me from going after my goals, dreams, and desires?*
- *What part of me doesn't believe in my full potential, and where did that belief originate?*

- *Why do I feel unworthy or afraid of success, and how can I heal this fear?*

These questions are designed to invite your superconscious mind to bring up the fragments that need attention and healing. It's important to remain patient as you wait for responses—often, the answers will come in subtle ways, such as intuitive insights, memories, or emotions that surface during the process.

Step 3: Engage in Direct Communication

Once you begin receiving answers, it's essential to engage with your fragmented self. The superconscious mind acts as a bridge between you and the fragmented parts of your personality. It can help facilitate communication with these aspects of yourself and guide them toward reintegration. For example, if you find that a part of you fears being seen or heard, ask that part: *What do you need to feel safe and confident?*

Invite the fragmented self to share its concerns, fears, and memories. Don't judge or rush through this process. Instead, offer a space of compassion and understanding.

The superconscious mind can help you reframe these fears, heal the underlying wounds, and reintegrate these fragments into your whole self.

Step 4: Reaffirm Your Power and Alignment

After speaking to your fragmented self, the next step is to reaffirm your power and commit to alignment. Ask your superconscious mind to help you bring these fragmented parts of yourself into harmony. Say something like:

I acknowledge all parts of me, even the ones that have been fragmented by fear or doubt. I call on my superconscious mind to help me heal, reintegrate, and become whole again. I choose to align with my true self, to embrace my full potential, and to live in harmony with all aspects of who I am.

By consciously inviting your superconscious mind into the process of healing, you are signaling to your brain and body that you are ready to embrace your full potential. This allows you to tap into a higher state of awareness, one that transcends the limitations of the past and moves you toward the future you desire.

Step 5: Reclaim Your Inner Power

The final step in this process is to **reclaim your inner power**. Healing the fragmented self is not just about resolving past wounds; it's about taking control of your future and aligning your actions with your true essence. Through the guidance of your superconscious mind, you can rewrite the stories of your life, heal past trauma, and step fully into the person you are meant to be.

By speaking directly to the fragmented parts of yourself using the superconscious mind, you can heal the emotional wounds that have kept you stuck and create the life you've always wanted.

The superconscious mind, when accessed and trusted, has the power to bring all the parts of you back together, to transform limiting beliefs into empowering ones, and to guide you on a path of continuous growth and self-empowerment.

Why It Works

This process works because the superconscious mind has an inherent understanding of who you truly are and what you are capable of. It has no attachment to the limiting beliefs or fears that might dominate your conscious mind. By using this higher consciousness to guide the healing of your fragmented self, you are engaging in a transformative process that works at the core of your being.

As you begin to reintegrate the fragments of yourself, you will notice a greater sense of wholeness and alignment. You will feel empowered to pursue your dreams, free from the fears and limiting beliefs that once held you back. The fragmented self will no longer have power over you, as you bring all aspects of yourself into harmony.

Healing the fragmented self through the superconscious mind is one of the most profound tools you can use to unlock your full potential and create the reality you desire.

Becoming One with Your Tasks

Henry David Thoreau once wrote, "If one advances confidently in the direction of his dreams, and endeavors to live the life which he has imagined, he will meet with unexpected success in common hours." This timeless wisdom reminds us that success isn't always about grand gestures or complex strategies.

Sometimes, it's about aligning yourself with your dreams and taking consistent, focused action. When you begin to truly merge with your tasks—when you see your work as an extension of your purpose and yourself—you unlock the potential to achieve extraordinary success in the everyday moments of life.

So how can you break free from the limiting beliefs and fragmented parts of yourself that prevent you from fully stepping into this flow? How can you heal and reintegrate the fragmented parts of your personality that are holding you back from fully embracing your goals?

Here's a step-by-step guide to help you do just that.

Steps to Eliminate Old Beliefs and Heal Your Fragmented Self

1. **Recognize that you're blocked.**

    The first step is acknowledging that something is standing in your way. There's an unconscious part of you that is preventing you from moving forward. Whether it's fear, doubt, or a sense of unworthiness, the first step to healing is simply recognizing that you're being blocked.

2. **Ask to communicate with the aspect of yourself that is holding you back.**

   The next step is to ask to speak with the part of your personality that is limiting your progress. Often, this part of yourself has a belief or fear that you're not consciously aware of. Ask, *"Why am I holding myself back from pursuing my goals?"* By asking this question, you open the door to dialogue with the part of you that has been limiting your potential.

3. **Engage in a conversation with that aspect of yourself.**

   Once you've identified the fragment of your personality that is causing you to feel stuck, engage with it as if you were talking to another person.

   You might be surprised at the insights that come through. Name this aspect of yourself—perhaps it's your "inner critic," "the doubter," or "the fearful one."

   This step of personifying the issue can help you separate it from your identity and give you the power to address it.

4. **Understand the belief.**

   Ask the part of you that's holding you back: *"What is the belief you hold, and where did it come from?"*

   You might discover that it originated from childhood experiences, societal conditioning, or past failures. Understanding the root of the belief allows you to gain perspective on its limitations and recognize that it no longer serves you.

5. **Express gratitude for the aspect of yourself that wants healing.**

   It may seem counterintuitive to be grateful for the parts of you that seem to be limiting your growth. But these fragments of yourself often developed as a way of protecting you, even if that protection no longer serves your highest good. Express gratitude to these aspects of your personality for their role in your journey, and acknowledge that they are now ready to heal and reintegrate with the whole of you.

6. **Release the limiting aspects of yourself.**

   Once you've understood the belief and expressed gratitude, give yourself permission to release the fragmented parts of yourself that are holding you back. Say to yourself, *"I no longer need this belief. I am who I say I am, and I can do what I say I can do."* This affirmation of self-trust and power is the key to shifting your reality and aligning with your true potential.

7. **Commit to your goals, no matter the obstacles.**

   The final step in this process is to commit. Commit to doing whatever it takes to turn your goals and dreams into reality.

It doesn't matter what obstacles you face along the way; this is about your unwavering dedication to your purpose.

As you continue to heal and integrate your fragmented self, you will find the strength to face challenges head-on and move forward with confidence.

This exercise may feel redundant and a bit strange at first, especially if you've never tried talking to yourself in this way. But remember, any discomfort or resistance you feel could be a sign of an old, outdated belief trying to hold you back. As you practice this process, you'll experience growth and transformation. The key to change is not merely thinking differently but shifting your internal dialogue and taking action.

From Thinking to Doing: The Power of Action

You can think about your dreams and goals all day long, but until you take action, nothing will change. The shift from thinking to doing is crucial if you want to turn your visions into reality. Why is action so powerful? Because action forces the mind and body to align with your dreams. There's something transformative about taking a physical step in the direction of your dreams. Once you make that first move, the universe begins to respond.

When you focus on what matters most—your dreams, your goals, your deepest desires—something remarkable happens. Everything else that doesn't serve your highest purpose begins to fade into the background. The more you act on your goals, the more the distractions, doubts, and fears fall away. You become more aligned with your true self, and the energy around you begins to support your efforts.

The Next Step: Manifesting Wealth and Success

In the next chapter, we will delve deeper into how you can manifest not just the life you want, but the **wealth** and **success** you deserve. By continuing to align with your true self and taking action, you can create the life you've always envisioned. The journey of personal transformation is ongoing, but every step you take brings you closer to the reality you've always dreamed of.

And with the steps outlined here, you'll be ready to unlock your full potential and manifest your deepest desires.

Success is not about luck. It's about alignment. When you align your thoughts, actions, and beliefs with your true purpose, success becomes an inevitable outcome.

This journey of healing and becoming one with your tasks is the foundation of everything you wish to create. Stay focused, stay committed, and trust the process, because you are more than capable of creating the life you've always dreamed of.

In Chapter 8, you'll learn how to apply the principles of manifestation to create the wealth and success you desire. This chapter focuses on aligning your thoughts, actions, and energy to attract opportunities and achieve your goals.

Here's what you'll learn:

- The Principles of Manifestation: Understand the science and mindset behind manifestation and how it relates to your goals.

- Clarifying Your Desires: Learn how to define what wealth and success mean to you with clarity and specificity.

- Aligning Thoughts and Actions: Discover how to combine positive thinking with intentional actions to create real results.

- The Role of Gratitude: Explore how cultivating gratitude amplifies your ability to attract abundance.

- Overcoming Scarcity Mindset: Identify and eliminate limiting beliefs about money and success that hold you back.

- Visualization and Affirmation Techniques: Master practical tools to keep your mind focused on your desired outcomes.

- Attracting Opportunities: Learn how to recognize and act on the opportunities that align with your vision for wealth and success.

By the end of this chapter, you'll have a clear roadmap for harnessing the power of manifestation, breaking through limiting beliefs, and building a life filled with abundance, prosperity, and fulfillment.

HOW TO MANIFEST WEALTH AND SUCCESS

"Success is not just about what you achieve, but about what you dare to believe and work relentlessly toward."

— *Unknown*

You were born with the potential to be healthy, wealthy, and wise—these are not just dreams or desires, they are your birthright. You are meant to have the life you've always envisioned, filled with abundance and success. Yet, the reason many of us don't achieve this dream is because of a limiting belief system—specifically, a negative money mindset. To manifest wealth and success, the first and most crucial step is to transform your mindset about money.

The Foundation of Wealth: Money Mindset

Everything you hope to achieve in life, from financial abundance to career success, ultimately comes down to your beliefs. What you believe is possible, what you feel you deserve, and most importantly, what you think you're worth—these beliefs dictate your reality.

If you believe that money flows to you effortlessly, if you view wealth as something abundant and deserving of you, then you will begin to attract it. Your inner energy will match that of prosperity, and opportunities will flow naturally into your life.

The key to unlocking financial success is simple: **you must believe in your own value.**

When you project that money loves you and you feel good about receiving wealth, that energy is mirrored back to you. You become a magnet for prosperity. So, the first thing to do in your quest for wealth is to heal and nurture your relationship with money. Change the narrative in your mind, and soon enough, the external world will align with your inner beliefs.

Mastery: The Key to Wealth and Success

Once your money mindset has shifted, it's time to get to work. To manifest wealth and success, you must become an expert in your field. Why? Because wealth and success are built on your ability to solve problems. And the more problems you solve, the more value you provide, and the more you earn. If you can solve a problem better than anyone else, people will pay for your solution.

Therefore, the first practical step towards wealth creation is to master your craft. Become so proficient and knowledgeable that your expertise becomes indispensable. This mastery is what separates you from the crowd and allows you to offer something unique that others are willing to pay for.

Value and Pricing: The Exchange of Goods

Now that you've mastered your craft, the next step is determining the value of what you offer and how much to charge. When you price your service or product, you're not just putting a number on something—you're acknowledging the value you're bringing into the world. And people will only pay you when they can see and feel the tangible benefits of what you're offering.

To understand this, consider three key factors:

1. **The Problems You Solve**

   Wealth is built on solving problems. The greater the problem you solve, the more you can charge for your solution. Identify the challenges your target audience is facing, and tailor your offerings to address these needs effectively.

2. **The Value You Provide**

   Your value is not just in the product or service you offer, but in how it changes lives. The deeper the transformation or benefit you provide, the more people will be willing to pay.

3. **How You Package and Deliver Your Offer**

   How you present your solution matters. People won't buy just because you offer something—they'll buy when they feel that your product is worth the price and delivers the desired value in a way that's easy for them to access. Packaging your expertise in a clear, accessible, and compelling way is key to making sales.

These three elements—solving problems, delivering value, and strategic packaging—are the foundation of any successful wealth-building venture. However, to truly succeed, you need to understand why people buy and, more importantly, why they don't.

Why People Don't Buy (And How to Change That)

Purchasing decisions are influenced by something called the *Stop/Go principle*. This principle states that every potential customer has an internal *Stop* signal and a *Go* signal. If the Stop signal is stronger, the person will not make the purchase. But if the Go signal is stronger, they'll be compelled to buy. The challenge for any entrepreneur is to increase the strength of the Go signal and minimize the Stop signal.

The Stop signal is usually triggered by doubt, fear, or disbelief—concerns like *"Is this worth the price?"* or *"I'm not sure if this will really solve my problem."*

On the other hand, the Go signal is activated when a person sees the clear value in what you're offering. They understand the benefits, trust in its effectiveness, and feel a sense of urgency to act.

To ensure the Go signal is stronger than the Stop signal, you must demonstrate the value of your offering clearly and convincingly.

People are more likely to buy from you if they see that your product is rare, of high quality, or will lead to a significant transformation in their lives.

Crafting an Irresistible Offer

Before you create something to sell, you must ask yourself: "Is this product or service something that my potential customers are willing to pay for? Does it solve a problem in a way that is valuable to them?" If the answer is yes, then you're on the right track. But if there's hesitation or doubt, this is your cue to refine your offering. Make sure that the value is undeniable and that the benefits are clearly communicated.

Your customers are not just purchasing a product—they are buying a solution to their problems. They are investing in the promise that your offering will make their lives better, easier, or more fulfilling. Therefore, ensure that your marketing and communication align with their desires and needs.

Conclusion: The Path to Manifesting Wealth and Success

To manifest wealth and success, you must first align your mindset with abundance and prosperity. Then, through mastery, you must offer value by solving the problems of others. Understand the psychology of your customers—their Stop and Go signals—and craft an offer that triggers the Go signal, leading them to take action and make a purchase.

Wealth is not a matter of luck or happenstance. It's a direct result of your mindset, your ability to solve problems, and your skill in packaging and delivering value. When you combine these elements, you unlock the potential to create wealth and success, not just for yourself, but for others as well.

The key to manifesting wealth and success is simple: become the solution to someone's problem, and they will happily pay for your expertise.

In Chapter 9, you'll discover the art of presenting yourself with confidence, authenticity, and value. This chapter will teach you how to communicate your unique story, skills, and vision in a way that resonates with others and opens doors to new opportunities.

Here's what you'll learn:

- **Understanding Your Value:** Learn how to identify and articulate your unique strengths, skills, and experiences.

- **Crafting Your Personal Brand:** Discover how to create a compelling narrative that showcases who you are and what you stand for.

- **Telling Your Story Effectively:** Master the art of storytelling to connect emotionally with others and make a lasting impression.

- **Communicating with Confidence:** Explore strategies to speak with clarity, assertiveness, and enthusiasm in any setting.

- **Building Relationships That Matter:** Learn how to establish trust and rapport with others, creating genuine and meaningful connections.

- **Overcoming Imposter Syndrome:** Develop the mindset to present yourself without fear, self-doubt, or hesitation.

- **Presenting Yourself in Different Contexts:** Adapt your messaging to suit interviews, networking events, public speaking, and online platforms.

By the end of this chapter, you'll have the tools to effectively sell yourself, inspire others, and open doors to the opportunities that align with your vision for success.

HOW TO SELL YOURSELF TO OTHERS

'If we all did the things we are capable of doing, we would literally astound ourselves.'

–Thomas A. Edison

Before you can sell yourself successfully—to sell your ideas, your products, your skills, your services—you must first be 100% sold on yourself. Why? Because nothing ever sells without a buyer, and no one will buy from you until you understand their needs and can see yourself from their perspective. **You must believe in yourself before others will believe in you.**

Selling yourself requires faith, confidence, and a deep understanding that success is about getting results for others. It's about seeing yourself as competent, likable, and resourceful—someone who knows how to communicate their message in a way that resonates with those they seek to serve.

To truly sell yourself, you must develop the confidence to show up as your authentic self and prove to others that you can help solve their problems. This authenticity creates trust, and trust is the foundation of any successful sale.

By the end of this guide, you will not only know how to craft a system for selling yourself but also how to present it in a way that works for you and your audience. **Learning how to sell yourself is one of the most important skills for success.**

Don't Fake It Until You Make It

You've likely heard the saying, "fake it till you make it," but in reality, it's not about pretending or deceiving others into believing you're something you're not. Instead, it's about utilizing the knowledge, skills, and expertise you already have to set yourself apart. The goal is not to fool anyone but to convince others that you can solve their problems better than anyone else can.

This mindset shift involves developing a positive attitude, seeing yourself as a leader, and positioning yourself as an expert who understands the needs of the people you aim to serve. You don't just want to sell; you want to create a *win-win* scenario where both you and your customer benefit.

Put Yourself in Their Shoes

To sell yourself effectively, you must first step into your potential customer's world. Understand their needs, desires, and pain points. Before you can sell yourself on your ideas, you must understand what matters to the person you are trying to help. By putting yourself in their shoes, you can better communicate how your solution aligns with their goals.

People can sense sincerity. When your intentions are genuine, they are far more likely to trust you and engage with your offerings. Demonstrating that you truly care about their concerns—not just about making a sale—builds trust. When people see that you have their best interests at heart, they become more confident in your ability to help them.

One of the biggest barriers to sales is the buyer's concern about what will happen after they make the purchase. They may wonder if you will be there to support them, follow through, and provide the help they need after the transaction is complete.

This is why empathy is essential. By understanding your customer's journey, you gain the perception necessary to reassure them that buying from you is a sound decision. People are often afraid of making the wrong choice, but when you show them that you genuinely understand their needs, you alleviate that fear.

Everything Is Energy

The first step in selling yourself is to examine the energy you project into the world. **Why? Because everything in life can be reduced to energy and vibrations.** At a subatomic level, there are no particles, only frequencies and energy. We are all either the cause or the effect of this energy.

Before you can sell yourself, you must become aware of the energy you radiate. Why? Because your energy either draws people to you or pushes them away. You've probably heard the saying, "People do business with people they know, like, and trust." If the energy you're projecting doesn't align with the energy your potential customers are seeking, you won't be able to sell to them.

According to the Universal Law of Cause and Effect, we get back what we put out. If you project negative energy, whether through doubt, frustration, or pessimism, you will attract that same energy back. But if you radiate positivity, confidence, and trustworthiness, you'll naturally attract those who resonate with your energy. Energy is the force that drives action—both yours and others'.

Why People Buy in the First Place

To sell yourself effectively, you must understand **why people buy.** What motivated them to make purchases in the past? What worked for them, and what didn't? By understanding their previous experiences, you can identify the gaps in their expectations and position your offering as the solution they need.

People are more likely to buy when they believe your product or service offers a solution that aligns with their desires. They want to feel that you are competent and trustworthy and that you can help them achieve their goals. Your job is to show them that you are the right choice.

Emotional Triggers and Their Role in Buying Decisions

Purchasing decisions are often driven by emotion, not logic. Why? Because emotions bypass rational thinking and tap into deeper instincts—like gut feelings. When people make a buying decision, it's often because they believe that the product or service will make them feel happier, more fulfilled, safer, or more successful.

As a communicator, your goal is to connect with these emotions. Understand your customer's world from their point of view, and show them how your offering can improve their life. **"No one cares how much you know until they know how much you care."** This is a critical lesson in sales: before you can influence someone's decision, you must first help them see the value in what you offer. Demonstrate that what you're providing will positively impact their lives, and they will feel more confident in their decision to buy from you.

Conclusion: The Art of Selling Yourself

Selling yourself is not about manipulation or persuasion—it's about authentic connection. It's about understanding the needs and emotions of the person you're engaging with, projecting the right energy, and offering something that solves a problem in a meaningful way. **The essence of selling is showing others that you genuinely care and that you can help them achieve their goals.**

By putting yourself in the other person's shoes, understanding the reasons behind their buying decisions, and using your energy to build trust and confidence, you can sell yourself successfully.

When you align your intentions with the needs of your audience and show them that you are the solution they've been looking for, you will create a deep, lasting connection that leads to success—for both you and your customers.

Crafting Your Solution: The Key to Winning Customers

When someone is considering a purchase, they're not just evaluating what you're offering; they're mentally processing three critical questions that will ultimately shape their decision:

1. Will this be worth it for me? *(Resonance)*

2. Is this the best option to help me achieve my goals? *(Differentiation)*

3. Can I do this on my own, or do I need help? *(Substantiation)*

Your ability to answer these questions in a compelling, clear, and persuasive way will directly impact whether you win the sale or lose it. But before we dive into how to craft that solution, it's crucial to understand where your potential customer's mind is when making these decisions.

Understanding Your Customer's State of Mind

Before your customer makes a buying decision, they are considering **where they are right now** versus **where they want to be.** They are asking themselves: *Is this the right fit for me? Will it take me closer to my desired outcome?*

At this point, they are not just evaluating your product or service; they're evaluating the effort required from them, compared to the support you will provide. This includes:

- **Who does what?** What is the role of the customer, and what will you, as the provider, be responsible for?

- **What are the expected outcomes at each phase?** What are the milestones of success?

- **How will they measure success?** How will they know they're on the right path?

These questions are fundamental because **clarity is key** to building trust and facilitating a confident buying decision. You must be able to paint a picture that shows them exactly what success will look like if they choose to work with you.

The Importance of Your Success Matrix

This is where **your Success Matrix** comes into play. Your Success Matrix is a visual, step-by-step plan that lays out the journey from where your customers are now to where they want to be. It's how you guide them through the process, showing them exactly how you're going to help them get the results they desire.

Why is this so important? **People only make decisions when they can clearly see the path forward.** They want to understand the sequence of events, the support they will receive, and the outcomes they can expect. Without this clarity, they'll hesitate, and their decision-making will be clouded by uncertainty.

You need to ensure they can easily grasp the transformation they will undergo after working with you. This process isn't just about outlining steps—it's about creating a mental model that aligns with their existing beliefs and knowledge. When people hear something unfamiliar or difficult to visualize, they instinctively resist. They might think:

- "This isn't for me."
- "This won't help me."

Their minds will choose the **path of least resistance**—what feels familiar and safe. So, your job is to show them that what you're offering is both **effective** and **aligned** with their current needs and that the old ways of doing things no longer serve their purpose.

Communicating Change and Transformation

When proposing something new or unfamiliar, you need to explicitly show that the past methods or solutions they have tried are no longer sufficient. What they've done before hasn't worked—or at least hasn't worked in the way they hoped. This doesn't mean belittling what's come before, but rather **illustrating why the current solution doesn't fit the problem anymore.**

At this moment, you must clearly define your role and explain how you're going to support them through the transition. **Support is key**—people need to feel reassured that they will not be left alone in the process. They need to trust that you will guide them every step of the way, so they don't feel lost or abandoned.

Your solution must provide **clarity and certainty** about the results they can expect. This is where the details matter: **How will they know they are succeeding?** Without clear indicators of success, it's easy for the customer to question whether the decision is worth it.

The Power of Clear Communication

When people are unclear about what the outcome will be, it becomes much harder to inspire them to take action. You must remove any doubt about the results they will experience. Be specific. Be precise. Show them that your solution is the **most efficient and effective path** to getting the results they want.

This is why clear communication is so essential in the sales process. **Your customer needs to understand how your offering will help them achieve their desired results.** Only then will they feel confident enough to move forward.

The Next Steps

In Chapter 10, you'll learn how to surround yourself with the right people and create a team that supports your vision, values, and goals. This chapter focuses on building strong relationships, fostering collaboration, and empowering others to achieve collective success.

Here's what you'll learn:

- **The Importance of a Strong Team:** Understand why no one achieves greatness alone and the role a supportive team plays in your success.

- **Identifying Key Roles and Skills:** Learn how to identify the strengths and skills you need in a team and how to find the right people who complement your abilities.

- **Effective Recruitment Strategies:** Discover how to attract and hire the right individuals who align with your vision and culture.

- **Building Trust and Accountability:** Learn how to foster an environment of trust, transparency, and shared responsibility within your team.

- **Developing Team Dynamics:** Explore how to create a collaborative culture where every team member feels valued, empowered, and motivated.

- **Leadership and Empowerment:** Master the art of leading by example, inspiring others, and giving your team the tools and autonomy they need to thrive.

- **Conflict Resolution and Growth:** Learn strategies for handling conflicts and challenges within your team, turning them into opportunities for growth and development.

By the end of this chapter, you'll be equipped with the knowledge and tools to build a high-performing team that not only supports your vision but also contributes to its ongoing growth and success.

10

BUILD AND DEVELOP A TEAM

"A man should first direct himself in the way he should go. Only then should he instruct others."

—*Buddha*

To build your dream team, you must first become a **visionary leader**. Why? Because visionary leaders possess the rare ability to see what others can't—the big picture. They're not bogged down by momentary setbacks or distractions. Instead, they perceive the opportunities hidden in every challenge, fueling their drive and perseverance even when the road gets tough.

But here's the key: visionary leaders don't keep their dreams to themselves. They **articulate** their vision with clarity and conviction, inspiring others to join in. When a leader's vision aligns with their **authentic self**—their core beliefs, values, and purpose—it resonates deeply with others. And that resonance? That's where team-building begins.

The Foundation of a Winning Team

The first step in building an effective and productive team is to **embrace your role as a supportive and effective leader**. What does that look like? It means creating a **win-win** environment where every team member feels **valued** and **empowered** to succeed. When people feel supported and recognized for their contributions, they are not just working for you—they are championing your cause.

They become invested in the mission. Compare this to a non-supportive leader, one who is self-absorbed and unwilling to consider others' perspectives. Such leaders miss out on the opportunity to turn dreams into reality because they fail to foster collaboration and trust.

But when you focus on building **relationships**, inspiring others, and offering **genuine support**, you unlock the first key to building an **unstoppable team**. Why? Because people are more likely to buy into your vision when they see how it benefits them, too.

As **Zig Ziglar** famously said, *"You can get everything in life you want if you will just help enough other people get what they want."*

Your Role as a Coach and Leader

Your job as a coach, teacher, and trainer is simple: **help others achieve their goals, and they'll help you achieve yours**. But here's the catch—it all begins with you.

First, you must **formulate a clear, compelling vision for yourself**. Once you've done that, you communicate that vision in a way that **inspires trust** and **belief**. People are drawn to leaders they trust and those who have their best interests at heart. When you communicate your vision effectively, others will realize that joining you isn't just about helping you succeed—it's about **fulfilling their own dreams**, too.

Good leaders don't just dictate; they **set the example**. They create an environment where team members feel **empowered, equipped**, and **confident** to contribute.

Why? Because people want to be part of something **bigger than themselves**, something that feels **meaningful**. They want to make a difference, not just punch a clock.

Building a High-Performing Team

At the core of effective team-building is one fundamental principle: **put the right people in the right roles**. It's about aligning each individual's strengths, passions, and goals so that they can contribute in a way that feels natural, fulfilling, and impactful.

Before placing someone in a role, ask yourself these questions:

1. **Mission**: What's the purpose of this role? What impact will it have on the team and the organization as a whole?
2. **Strengths**: What talents, skills, and knowledge are essential for success in this role?
3. **Motivation**: Does this role align with the individual's passions, long-term goals, and personal values?
4. **Fit**: Does this person's character, style, and values align with the team's culture and dynamic?

Taking the time to assess **fit** early on is crucial. When a team is aligned—both in skills and values—it's a **powerful** and **cohesive** unit that works in harmony, driving forward with unstoppable momentum.

Aligning Goals to Maximize Success

Lastly, make sure your team's goals align with your overall **mission** and vision. When everyone is rowing in the same direction, you'll move faster and achieve more. A well-aligned team doesn't just work efficiently—they create a culture of collective success.

Aligning goals requires more than just ensuring everyone's tasks are clear. It means fostering a deep understanding of how individual roles contribute to the bigger picture.

When team members see how their work impacts the larger mission, they feel a stronger sense of ownership and commitment to the cause.

As a visionary leader, your job is to make sure everyone understands the **purpose** behind their work, how it fits into the team's success, and how it contributes to the achievement of the mission.

Final Thoughts: The Power of Building the Right Team

Building a dream team is not an accident. It's the result of strategic leadership, intentional support, and a clear, compelling vision. As a leader, your role is to inspire, guide, and empower your team to become the best version of themselves. By focusing on aligning individual strengths with the overall mission, you create an environment where everyone feels valued, motivated, and ready to succeed.

When you become the leader who builds the right culture, fosters trust, and inspires passion, you won't just achieve your goals—you'll exceed them, creating a legacy of success that others will want to be a part of.

So, as you embark on this journey, remember: that **great teams are not built overnight**. But with patience, dedication, and a clear vision, you'll turn your dream team into a reality. Let's keep moving forward—one step, one leader, one team at a time.

Start a Meetup Group

Starting a Meetup group can be a powerful way to build your network, share your vision, and achieve your goals, dreams, and desires.

Meetup groups aren't just about gathering people in a room—they're about creating meaningful connections, fostering collaboration, and building a community that champions your mission. Whether you want to promote a business, share knowledge, or create social impact, a well-run Meetup group can accelerate your success. Here's how to start and run one effectively.

Step 1: Define Your Purpose

Before you create a Meetup group, clarify its purpose. Ask yourself:

- What is the ultimate goal of this group?
- Who is my ideal member? What are their needs and interests?
- How does this group align with my personal or professional goals?

For example, if you're an entrepreneur, your group might focus on networking and skill-building for like-minded professionals.

If you're a coach or trainer, your group could provide workshops or discussions that align with your expertise.

Step 2: Choose a Specific Niche

Who you are at your core should guide the niche you choose for your Meetup group.

Your unique identity and experiences will naturally attract the right people and foster a sense of belonging. Instead of starting a generic "Networking Group," align your group with your authentic self.

For instance, if you're passionate about empowering women in technology, you might start a "Women Entrepreneurs in Tech" group. Or, if mindfulness and outdoor adventure are central to your identity, consider a "Weekend Hikers and Mindfulness Practitioners" group.

By declaring who you are and what you stand for, your niche will resonate deeply, making your group stand out in a crowded market.

Step 3: Set Up Your Meetup Group Profile

On Meetup.com, your group's profile is your first impression. Make it compelling and informative:

1. **Group Name:** Choose a name that reflects your mission and appeals to your target audience.

2. **Description:** Write a clear and engaging description. Include what members can expect, the group's purpose, and any unique benefits.

3. **Visuals:** Use a professional or eye-catching image for your group logo and banner.

4. **Topics and Tags:** Add relevant keywords and categories to make it easier for potential members to find your group.

Step 4: Plan and Host Your First Meetup

Your first event sets the tone for your group, so make it count. Here's how:

- **Choose a Format:** Decide if your Meetup will be in-person, virtual, or hybrid. Formats might include workshops, panel discussions, social mixers, or hands-on activities.

- **Pick the Right Venue:** For in-person events, choose a location that's accessible and aligns with your group's vibe. For virtual events, select a reliable platform like Zoom or Google Meet.

- **Create a Detailed Agenda:** Outline what will happen at the event. A structured agenda keeps things organized and ensures a positive experience.

- **Market Your Event:** Use social media, email newsletters, and word-of-mouth to spread the word. Be sure to invite friends and colleagues to build initial momentum.

Step 5: Foster Engagement and Build Relationships

Building a successful Meetup group isn't just about attendance numbers—it's about creating a community. Focus on:

- **Welcoming New Members:** Greet new attendees personally, introduce them to others, and make them feel included.

- **Facilitating Connection:** Encourage group discussions, networking opportunities, and collaborative projects.

- **Gathering Feedback:** After each event, ask members what they liked and what could be improved. Use this feedback to refine future Meetups.

Step 6: Be Consistent

Consistency is key to maintaining interest and engagement. Schedule regular Meetups—monthly or bi-weekly—and stick to your schedule. Members are more likely to stay active if they know they can rely on your group to meet consistently.

Step 7: Collaborate and Grow

As your group grows, consider:

- **Partnering with Others:** Collaborate with local businesses, influencers, or organizations to provide value and expand your reach.

- **Inviting Guest Speakers:** Bring in experts who can offer unique insights and attract new members.

- **Diversifying Events:** Mix up your formats to keep things fresh, such as hosting webinars, Q&A sessions, or themed activities.

Step 8: Monetize (If Appropriate)

If your group aligns with your professional goals, consider ways to monetize your efforts:

- **Event Fees:** Charge a small fee for premium events.

- **Sponsorships:** Partner with companies that want to reach your audience.

- **Promote Your Services:** Subtly introduce your offerings (e.g., coaching, courses, or consulting) in a way that adds value to your members.

Step 9: Track Your Success

Measure your progress by evaluating:

- **Attendance:** How many people are showing up?

- **Engagement:** Are members actively participating in and sharing feedback?

- **Growth:** Is your group's membership steadily increasing?

- **Impact:** Are you achieving the goals you set for yourself and helping members achieve theirs?

Step 10: Stay Authentic

The most successful Meetup groups are led by people who are genuine, passionate, and invested in their mission. Be approachable, transparent, and authentic in your interactions. When members sense your sincerity, they're more likely to stay engaged and loyal.

Starting and running a successful Meetup group takes effort, but the rewards—from expanding your network to achieving your goals—are well worth it.

Remember, it's not just about gathering people; it's about creating a community that shares a vision and works together to bring it to life.

In Chapter 11, you'll learn how to develop a market strategy that positions you and your offerings for maximum visibility, impact, and profitability. This chapter will guide you through the process of identifying your target market, crafting your message, and developing a plan to reach and engage your ideal audience.

Here's what you'll learn:

- **Defining Your Target Market:** Learn how to identify and understand the specific audience you want to serve—what they need, want, and struggle with.

- **Crafting Your Unique Value Proposition:** Discover how to communicate the unique value you bring to the table in a way that resonates deeply with your audience.

- **Positioning Yourself in the Market:** Understand how to carve out your niche, differentiate yourself from competitors, and stand out in a crowded marketplace.

- **Building Your Brand Message:** Learn how to craft a compelling brand message that speaks directly to the desires and pain points of your ideal customers.

- **Creating a Multi-Channel Marketing Plan:** Explore strategies to use various platforms—social media, email, content marketing, and more—to reach and engage your audience.

- **Engaging and Nurturing Your Audience:** Learn how to build relationships with your audience by providing consistent value, building trust, and nurturing leads into loyal customers.

- **Measuring and Adjusting Your Strategy:** Discover how to track the success of your marketing efforts, analyze results, and adapt your strategy for continuous improvement.

By the end of this chapter, you'll have a clear, actionable market strategy to reach your ideal customers, build your brand's presence, and create long-term success in your industry.

CREATE YOUR MARKET STRATEGY

"When you change the way you look at things, the things you look at change."

—*Anonymous*

Now that we've covered a lot of foundational concepts in this book, it's time to put it all together into a **market strategy**. Why? Because as dynamic and creative as you are, your ideas and offerings won't gain traction unless they're seen and heard. And let's be honest: in today's world, attracting clients and generating income isn't easy. With the average attention span now under five seconds, the real challenge is figuring out how to stand out in a crowded marketplace.

People are constantly juggling multiple responsibilities, and they're bombarded with distractions from all sides. So, what can you do to capture their attention and get them to notice what you have to offer? You might even wonder, how can you leverage your time and energy to attract new clients when it feels like there's always more to do and not enough hours in the day?

The answer lies in **creating a robust marketing system**.

The Power of a Marketing System

Why is a well-designed marketing system so important? Because it allows you to **work on your business**, not just **on** it. You'll no longer be constantly scrambling to create content or find new leads.

Instead, your marketing system will function like a machine, bringing in clients day after day.

This approach doesn't just streamline your operations—it gives you the freedom to focus on the tasks that truly move the needle forward, helping you achieve that elusive **work-life balance**.

After all, you didn't start your business to sacrifice your health, relationships, or personal well-being. So, why spend endless hours on tasks that don't add significant value?

A successful marketing system is one that is **automated**—one that operates efficiently and effectively, without requiring constant oversight. Automation takes care of the repetitive tasks so that you and your team can focus on the human aspects of your business: creativity, strategy, customer relationships, and decision-making.

Why Automation Works

Automated systems are powerful tools that can transform your business operations. Here's why:

1. **Efficiency**: Automated systems complete tasks quickly, accurately, and consistently—without the fatigue or errors that humans often experience.

2. **24/7 Operation**: Automation works around the clock, delivering results even when you're sleeping.

3. **Scalability**: As your business grows, automated systems can handle increased demands without needing to hire more staff. This makes them cost-effective, sustainable, and adaptable to the needs of your growing business.

4. **Consistency and Accuracy**: By performing tasks the same way every time, automated systems ensure consistent results, reducing human error and maintaining the quality of your work.

5. **Freeing Up Time**: With the routine tasks taken care of, your team can focus on high-value work that requires human ingenuity, such as customer service, brainstorming new ideas, and strategic planning.

Think of automation as a **well-oiled machine** that keeps your business running smoothly. It frees up your time and energy to focus on the things that truly matter.

How People See You

The first step in carving out your niche is determining **how** people will discover you. **Visibility** is key. If potential clients don't know who you are or what you offer, how can they choose to work with you?

If you want to build a thriving, million-dollar solo enterprise, you need to make your mark—and the best way to do that is through **social media**. Why is social media essential? Because it's not just a platform for advertising—it's a vibrant marketplace where your ideal clients already exist. These platforms allow you to **engage** with your audience and build relationships that go beyond surface-level interactions.

But here's the question: **Which platform will serve your business goals best?**

To make the most of social media, you must choose the platform that aligns with your goals and the needs of your target audience. Consider where your ideal customers spend their time and where they go to find solutions to their problems. The key is to connect with those who are genuinely interested in what you offer and who will appreciate the value you provide.

Building Trust Through Content

Once you've chosen the right platform, it's time to start **building trust** with your audience. One of the most effective ways to do this is by sharing valuable, **free content**.

This could be in the form of:

- Newsletters
- Blog posts
- Podcasts
- Webinars
- Social media posts

Sharing your knowledge for free allows potential clients to get to know you, trust you, and begin to see the value you provide. This is the **Know, Like, Trust** factor—the foundation of any successful marketing strategy.

By offering value upfront, you're not just selling your products or services; you're establishing yourself as a credible authority in your field. And once people trust you, they're more likely to invest in your paid offerings.

The Conversion Process

Now, once you've built that trust, it's time to transition to the next stage: **conversions**. When people know, like, and trust you, they're more likely to say "yes" when you offer them something. Whether it's a product, a service, or a program, they're already convinced of your expertise and the value you bring.

This is where your marketing system becomes vital. You want to be able to seamlessly guide potential clients from the discovery phase to the buying phase, without being overly pushy or salesy. Your system should provide clear, accessible paths for people to engage with your offerings, whether through a simple email sequence, a free trial, or an invitation to book a call.

Social Media as a Relationship Builder

Ultimately, social media is not just a tool for promotion; it's a **relationship builder**. It allows you to engage with your audience, build rapport, and share insights that position you as a trusted expert in your field. And when people trust you, they're more likely to make that leap from passive follower to active client.

The best way to use social media is to provide valuable content consistently. Share your knowledge, answer questions, and engage in meaningful conversations with your audience. As you do, you'll start to create a community of people who are eager to learn from you, invest in your offerings, and become loyal customers.

Final Thoughts: The Power of Visibility and Trust

Building a successful business isn't just about creating a great product or service—it's about making sure that people can **find you**, **understand** what you offer, and **trust** you. Your marketing system and social media presence should work in tandem to increase your visibility, foster trust, and build lasting relationships with your ideal clients.

By leveraging automation, creating valuable content, and consistently engaging with your audience, you'll be well on your way to not just attracting clients, but turning them into loyal, long-term customers who are eager to support your business growth. The time to start is now—let's make sure your marketing strategy is working for you, not against you.

Set up your digital presence with a website

Your online presence is often the first point of contact between you and potential clients. It's crucial to consider how you're represented on the internet and whether it accurately reflects your offerings and values. Creating a professional and engaging website is an excellent starting point.

A well-designed website serves multiple purposes - it's not just a platform for people to learn more about you and what you do, but also a powerful marketing tool that can enhance your brand's credibility.

A great website can help your customers feel confident about doing business with you. It's like a digital storefront that showcases your products or services, shares your story, and communicates your brand's values and mission. To create a website that truly resonates with your customers, you need to step into their shoes. Imagine they're visiting your website for the first time.

What impression do you want to leave them with? What actions do you want them to take? Perhaps you want them to browse your products, book a consultation, sign up for a newsletter, or simply learn more about your brand.

But more importantly, consider what would make them want to do business with you. Is it the quality of your products or services? Your brand's mission and values? Customer testimonials and reviews? Or perhaps it's your unique selling proposition that sets you apart from the competition?

Your website is like a vibrant, dynamic billboard that showcases who you are and what you offer, 24/7. It's a cost-effective marketing superhero! For a fraction of the cost, you can reach a global audience, update your content anytime, and track user engagement with precision. It's like having your very own marketing department that never sleeps.

Your website is your secret weapon, helping you stay competitive. It's your chance to stand out from the crowd, to show the world what makes you unique. With a well-designed, user-friendly website, you're not just keeping up with your competitors; you're setting the pace.

If your website isn't mobile-friendly, you're leaving money on the table. We're living in a world where people are glued to their phones 24/7.

They're browsing, shopping, and connecting with brands on the go. If your website doesn't look good or function well on a mobile device, you're going to lose out. Big time.

And here's the thing: it's not just about aesthetics.

It's about user experience. If your site isn't responsive, it's going to be a pain to navigate on a small screen.

People don't have the patience for that. They'll bounce. And guess what? You've just lost a potential customer.

But it's not just about the users. Google cares about this stuff too. If your site isn't mobile-friendly, it can hurt your search engine rankings. And you know what that means? Less visibility, less traffic, less business. It's a domino effect. So, make your website mobile-friendly. Make it responsive.

It's not a nice-to-have anymore. It's a must. Because the future of business is mobile, and you need to be ready for it.

Working with a Web Developer

When it comes to creating a website for your business, **working with a web developer** can be a game-changer. These experts are skilled at crafting websites that are not only visually stunning but also function seamlessly. But let's face it, hiring a professional comes with a cost. Depending on the complexity of the site and the rates of the developer, this could be an investment anywhere from a few hundred dollars to several thousand.

If you have the budget for it, this investment is usually worth it. A **professionally designed website** enhances your brand's image, improves user experience, and can drive more business your way. A skilled web developer will ensure that your site not only looks great but also performs well, providing an optimal experience for your visitors.

But what if you're working with a tight budget? Don't worry, there are plenty of cost-effective alternatives. Platforms like **Wix** and **WordPress** offer user-friendly website builders that require little to no technical knowledge. These platforms come with a range of templates and customization options, allowing you to create a professional-looking website that still reflects your brand's personality.

DIY Website Building

With tools like Wix or WordPress, you can easily add pages, upload content, and even integrate e-commerce features if you're planning to sell products or services online. These platforms offer different pricing plans to fit various needs and budgets, making it possible for nearly anyone to build a beautiful website.

If you're taking the DIY route, pay special attention to **design elements** such as color schemes, typography, layout, and navigation. These factors influence the **user experience** (UX) and can make or break how visitors perceive your brand.

Once you've identified a few websites you like (three or four should do the trick), use those as inspiration to start thinking about your own. What features do you want? What pages do you need? What content do you plan to include? And importantly, how much time are you willing to commit to maintaining the site after it's built?

Content Development and Brand Consistency

Once you've chosen your design and platform, the next step is **content development**. This is where many businesses run into trouble: assuming that the web developer will handle content creation. The reality is, that **content development is on you**. If your content isn't ready when the design is in progress, it could cause delays and even lead to redesigns once your developer starts integrating the text.

Here are some pages you'll want to focus on:

- **Homepage**: This is the first impression visitors get of your business. It needs to clearly convey what you do and what sets you apart.

- **Product or Services Pages**: Showcase what you're offering, providing clear details and call-to-action buttons that guide visitors to make a purchase or inquire further.

- **About Us**: Tell the story of your brand, and the values that drive you, and introduce your team. This is your opportunity to build trust with your audience.

- **Testimonials Page**: Social proof is crucial. Highlight positive feedback from your customers to reinforce credibility.

- **Contact Us**: Make it easy for visitors to reach out to you. Include forms, phone numbers, or email addresses.

- **Blog or News Section**: Keep your audience updated with relevant articles, news, and insights.

Remember, consistency is key. A unified **brand theme** across all pages helps solidify your identity and creates a memorable experience for your visitors. The **color palette, fonts**, and logo should align with the message you want to communicate about your business. When these elements are consistent, they foster trust and make your business more recognizable.

Establishing Your Brand Identity

Your **brand identity** is the heartbeat of your business. It goes beyond a logo or tagline—it's the essence of who you are, what you stand for, and how you're different from your competitors. Think of your brand as the story you tell the world about your company.

Your Logo: The Face of Your Brand

The logo is **the face of your brand**, and just like a person's face, it should be distinct and memorable. A well-designed logo grabs attention and leaves a lasting impression. Think of **Nike** or **Apple**—their logos are simple yet instantly recognizable.

When designing your logo, think about what values your business represents and how you can communicate those visually.

Focus on:

- **Simplicity**: A logo should be easy to recognize and reproduce.

- **Meaning**: Does the design reflect your company's core values?

- **Relevance**: Make sure it fits with the industry you're in.

Remember, your logo will be used on everything from your website to business cards, and even your products. It's the cornerstone of your brand.

Tangible Brand Touchpoints

Even in a digital world, **physical touchpoints** like business cards, letterheads, and envelopes still make a big impact. These items give your brand a tangible presence and can leave a lasting impression on clients and partners. Ensure that your stationery aligns with your online branding—use your logo, brand colors, and high-quality materials to maintain consistency and professionalism.

Driving Traffic to Your Site with SEO

Once you've created an amazing website, the next step is **driving traffic** to it. And that's where **Search Engine Optimization (SEO)** comes into play.

SEO is the art and science of improving your website's visibility on search engines like Google. When someone searches for a business or service like yours, you want to ensure that your website shows up on the **first page** of the search results.

Here's a simple analogy: Imagine you're a bakery in California, and you've just launched a website to showcase your delicious pastries. Now, if someone searches for "best bakery in California," you want your website to appear in those search results.

If you're not optimized for SEO, you could miss out on potential customers searching for exactly what you offer.

How SEO Works

SEO involves a variety of strategies, such as:

- **On-page SEO**: This includes optimizing your website content, like adding **relevant keywords**, using **engaging headers**, and ensuring your **images** are optimized for faster loading. For example, if you run a blog about healthy recipes, include keywords like "healthy recipes," "nutritious meals," or "diet-friendly desserts" in your content.

- **Off-page SEO**: Think of this as **word-of-mouth marketing**. It's all about **backlinks**—other reputable sites linking to yours. For example, if a popular food blog links to your bakery's website, that's a strong endorsement that can boost your site's credibility and ranking.

- **Technical SEO**: This is the behind-the-scenes work that makes sure your website functions smoothly. It includes things like ensuring fast **site speed** and making sure your site is **mobile-friendly**. If your site is slow or doesn't work well on smartphones, visitors will quickly leave, and that can hurt your ranking.

Why SEO is Critical

The goal of SEO is to ensure that **the right people** find your website. Good SEO practices bring in **targeted traffic**—people who are already interested in what you're offering. And more visitors mean more **potential customers**.

When done correctly, SEO can make your website more visible, increase traffic, and ultimately drive **sales** and **growth** for your business. It's not a one-time thing—SEO requires ongoing effort and adjustment, but once it's set up, it's a game-changer for your visibility and success.

In conclusion, SEO is an essential part of getting your website seen but remember: it's a marathon, not a sprint. Make sure your website is built on solid SEO principles, and you'll be well on your way to attracting the right audience to your business.

Generating Leads to Your Website Through Online Advertising

Online advertising has the potential to bring great results, but it's often met with mixed reviews. Some businesses swear by it, while others claim it's a waste of money. The truth lies somewhere in between—it depends on your business, audience, and how you approach it. I'm going to walk you through some popular options for online advertising, so you can decide which ones work best for your business.

Popular Online Advertising Options

1. Google AdWords (Pay-Per-Click Advertising)

Google AdWords is one of the most widely used online advertising platforms. It allows you to create **pay-per-click (PPC) ads** that show up in Google's search results when people search for specific keywords related to your business. For example, if you own a shoe store, you could bid on keywords like "running shoes" or "women's sneakers" to show your ad to people searching for those terms.

Advantages of Google AdWords:

- **Targeted Reach**: You're reaching people who are already actively searching for your product or service.

- **Control Over Budget**: You set your daily budget, so you decide how much you want to spend.

- **Quick Results**: Once you set up your ad, it can go live on Google in minutes.

However, keep in mind that you pay whether people click on your ad or not (if you choose **CPC**), or for every 1,000 impressions (if you use **CPM**). For those starting out with a tight budget, it might be better to try other, less expensive methods first.

2. Facebook Ads (Targeted Social Advertising)

If you're targeting a specific audience based on **demographics**, **interests**, and **location**, **Facebook Ads** could be an effective way to drive traffic. You can create ads that appear on Facebook, Instagram, Messenger, or Audience Network, giving you a wide reach across social platforms.

Advantages of Facebook Ads:

- **Precise Targeting**: You can target your audience based on age, gender, interests, behavior, and even specific online activity.

- **Variety of Ad Formats**: You can use images, videos, carousels, slideshows, and more to create engaging ads.

- **Budget Control**: Like Google AdWords, you can set a daily or lifetime budget and Facebook won't exceed it.

To get started, go to Facebook's **Ads Manager**. It will guide you through creating an ad with clear objectives, whether you want to build brand awareness, drive traffic, or increase conversions. The more you experiment with different ad formats, the better you'll understand what works for your business.

3. Display/Banner Ads (Visual Advertising)

Display ads are graphical advertisements that typically appear on websites. These ads can be static images or dynamic elements like animated GIFs and videos. They are great for **brand awareness**, as they focus on visual appeal to capture the attention of users as they browse various websites.

For instance, a **clothing brand** might use a high-quality image of its latest collection to entice potential customers, or a **fitness company** might run a short video showing off its workout equipment.

4. Key Advertising Terms

To better understand online advertising, here are two critical terms you'll encounter:

- **CPC (Cost Per Click)**: CPC refers to the amount you pay each time someone clicks on your ad.

   For example, if you set your CPC at $1, you'll pay $1 for every click. The goal is to get as many clicks as possible while staying within your budget.

- **CPM (Cost Per Thousand Impressions)**: CPM is the cost you pay for every 1,000 times your ad is shown, regardless of whether or not someone clicks on it. For example, if your CPM is $5, you'll pay $5 for every 1,000 impressions. This type of ad is more about visibility and brand awareness than immediate clicks.

If your main goal is to **increase visibility** or **brand awareness**, then CPM can be a more suitable option. However, if you're focusing on driving traffic to your website and getting people to take action (like signing up or purchasing), then **CPC** might be a better fit.

Which Type of Advertising is Right for Your Business?

The choice between these advertising options depends on your business model, your goals, and where your target audience hangs out. Here's a quick breakdown:

- **Google AdWords**: Great for businesses with **specific products or services** that people are actively searching for. It's perfect for those who want **immediate traffic** and are willing to pay for it.

- **Facebook Ads**: Perfect for businesses that benefit from **targeted marketing**, especially if you want to reach people based on their **interests** or **demographics**. It's a good choice if your products or services have a **broad appeal** or you're building brand awareness.

- **Display Ads**: Best for businesses looking to **visually engage** potential customers and increase **brand recognition**.

- These are ideal for companies with a **compelling visual product** or those seeking to **grow their audience** in specific markets.

Experiment, Track, and Optimize

Creating successful ads is not a one-size-fits-all solution. **Trial and error** will be a part of the process. The key is to **test** different strategies, measure the results, and **optimize** over time. Whether you're adjusting your **target audience**, changing your ad format, or tweaking your budget, experimentation will help you discover what works best for you.

Conclusion

Online advertising can be an incredibly effective way to **generate leads** and **drive traffic** to your website. But remember, it's not about spending as much as possible; it's about spending **smart**. Understand your audience, set clear goals, and continually refine your approach. When done right, online ads can fuel your business growth, leading to more conversions and higher sales.

Audio and Video Podcasts: Building Personal Connection and Expanding Your Reach

In today's digital age, podcasts have emerged as an incredibly effective way to **capture attention** and **engage an audience**. Why? Because consumers today crave content that is not only informative but also **dynamic** and **personal**. Whether through audio or video, podcasts give your audience a chance to feel closer to you—like you're speaking directly to them.

Why Podcasts Work:

- **Personal Connection**: Audio and video content allow your audience to hear your voice or see you in action. This humanizes your brand and builds a sense of **trust**.

  It's like inviting your audience into your life—showing them behind-the-scenes glimpses of who you are and what you do.

- **Shareability**: The beauty of podcasts is their **shareability**. Audio and video files are easy to share across social media platforms, spreading your message far and wide with just a click. That means your content has the potential to reach thousands or even millions of people without much extra effort.

- **Staying Power**: Unlike some fleeting trends, **multimedia content** is here to stay. As technology continues to evolve, podcasts and videos will only grow in importance as a means of communication and content consumption.

Whether it's **Spotify**, **Apple Podcasts**, or platforms like **Instagram**, **Facebook**, and **TikTok**, podcasts offer multiple ways to amplify your message and **expand your audience**.

Leveraging YouTube for Your Business: Making Your Brand Stand Out

YouTube isn't just a video-sharing platform; it's a **business powerhouse**. With over two billion logged-in monthly users, YouTube offers unparalleled access to potential customers. It allows you to create **dynamic** content that brings your brand to life in ways that text simply cannot.

Why YouTube is Great for Business:

- **Personal and Engaging Experience**: YouTube offers a visual and interactive experience that connects you with your audience in a personal way.

  You can showcase your products, demonstrate your services, and engage in storytelling that resonates with viewers.

- **Social Network Features**: YouTube is more than just a place to upload videos; it's a **social platform**. You can create a channel, interact with your followers, and link back to your website, giving your audience a place to explore more about your business.

- **Flexibility in Content Creation**: Even if you don't have the resources to upload new content every week, a **handful of well-crafted videos** can go a long way. The key is to **focus on quality over quantity**. You don't need a viral hit to succeed—moderate views can still generate meaningful business opportunities.

Creating Content for YouTube: Start by understanding your audience. What are their needs, challenges, and interests? **Address their pain points** with content that solves problems or educates them. If you're a fitness trainer, share workout routines. If you're a chef, offer cooking tips.

Share your journey, your **successes** and **failures**, as people love to connect with real, relatable stories. Ask your viewers for feedback, run polls, and keep the conversation going.

By engaging with your audience on YouTube, you're not just building your brand; you're also creating a **community**. This interaction helps you tailor your content and establish stronger relationships with your followers.

Building Business Connections with LinkedIn: Networking for Success

LinkedIn is more than just an online resume; it's a **professional networking powerhouse.**

As the go-to platform for **career advancement, business partnerships**, and **industry connections**, LinkedIn offers incredible potential for expanding your professional network.

What Makes LinkedIn Special:

- **Showcase Your Professional Story**: LinkedIn is a space where you can showcase more than just job titles. It's about telling your **professional story**, highlighting your **unique value proposition**, and positioning yourself as an expert in your field.

- **Building Connections**: Whether you're reconnecting with old colleagues or reaching out to industry leaders, LinkedIn helps you **connect** with people who can open doors to new opportunities.

- **Recommendations and Endorsements**: Your credibility is one of your greatest assets. Encouraging clients, colleagues, and peers to leave **recommendations** or **endorse skills** can help solidify your reputation and attract new opportunities.

But LinkedIn isn't just for job seekers, it's also a content platform. You can **share articles**, post updates, and engage with content from your connections. This helps you establish yourself as a **thought leader** in your industry while keeping your network up to date with your projects and insights.

Six Degrees of Separation on LinkedIn:

One of LinkedIn's most fascinating features is how it brings the concept of **six degrees of separation** to life. Through LinkedIn, you're not just connecting with individuals, you're also potentially accessing their **entire network**. When you connect with someone, you can view their **2nd-degree connections** (people they're connected to) and even **3rd-degree connections** (people connected to your 2nd-degree connections).

This means a simple connection could exponentially expand your reach, offering endless networking opportunities.

Imagine you connect with a colleague, and through them, you discover a potential business partner. LinkedIn turns **small connections** into **big opportunities**, allowing you to network strategically and unlock new professional relationships.

Conclusion

By incorporating **audio and video podcasts**, **YouTube videos**, and **LinkedIn networking** into your strategy, you can build a more **personal** and **engaging** brand presence that speaks directly to your audience. These platforms allow you to showcase your expertise, connect with potential clients, and amplify your message in ways that are **authentic** and **effective**. The key is to stay consistent, understand your audience's needs, and create content that provides value. The more you connect with your audience, the more they'll trust you—and that trust will translate into business growth.

In Chapter 12, you'll learn how to turn your plans into reality by taking consistent, massive action every single day. This chapter focuses on the power of daily, focused effort and how it accelerates progress toward your goals.

Here's what you'll learn:

- **The Power of Massive Action:** Understand why taking bold, consistent action is the key to making your vision a reality, and how it propels you forward even when challenges arise.

- **Breaking Through Resistance:** Learn how to overcome procrastination, fear, and self-doubt by committing to take action, regardless of how you feel in the moment.

- **Daily Habits for Success:** Discover the habits and routines that high achievers use to stay productive and focused on their goals each day.

- **Staying Accountable:** Explore strategies to hold yourself accountable and ensure you're consistently moving forward, even when motivation wanes.

- **Turning Action into Momentum:** Learn how to build momentum through small, consistent steps that compound over time, leading to massive results.

- **The Role of Adaptability:** Understand how to take massive action while remaining flexible and adjusting your strategy as you learn and grow.

- **Creating a Results-Oriented Mindset:** Shift your thinking from "planning" to "doing" and develop a mindset that prioritizes action as the pathway to success.

By the end of this chapter, you'll be equipped with the tools to take massive, focused action every day, turning your dreams into tangible results. You'll learn that action, not intention, is what truly moves you toward success.

GET MAD (MASSIVE ACTION DAILY)

"Success is the sum of small efforts, repeated day in and day out."

— *Robert Collier*

In this final chapter, we arrive at the cornerstone of achieving your dreams: **Massive Action Daily (MAD)**. MAD is more than just a motivational buzzword; it's the secret weapon that propels you toward your goals with unmatched focus and intensity. It's a day dedicated entirely to taking relentless, focused action to jump-start or re-energize your progress. The key to success lies in how consistently and boldly you apply yourself—and MAD is the formula that ensures you do.

Preparation for a MAD

The first step to making a MAD successful is ensuring you're fully prepared for it. As with any crucial task, preparation is essential.

1. **Focus on One Goal at a Time:**

   To truly make progress, you must channel your energy toward one specific goal during your MAD. The power of focus cannot be overstated. Imagine a beam of light—when scattered, its power weakens, but when concentrated, it has the strength to cut through steel. By focusing solely on one goal, you maximize your effort and eliminate distractions. If you have multiple goals, schedule separate MADs for each one, giving each the full attention it deserves.

2. **Schedule Your MAD in Advance:**

   A MAD day is not something you fit in between meetings or squeeze into a crowded calendar. It's a priority, and as such, it should be scheduled well in advance. Treat this time as sacred—like an important meeting with yourself. If committing an entire day feels overwhelming, begin with a **Massive Action Half Day (MAHD)** to test the waters.

3. **Gather Your Tools and Resources:**

   Don't squander your most productive hours gathering materials. The first couple of hours of your day are often when your energy and focus are at their peak. If you spend this time looking for tools or supplies, it's like filling a bucket with water only to have it leak away. Prepare everything you need beforehand to ensure your MAD day begins seamlessly.

4. **Insulate Yourself from Interruptions:**

   One of the biggest barriers to productivity is distraction. To safeguard your MAD, create an environment where interruptions are minimized. Turn off your phone, block off your calendar, and communicate with those around you. Let colleagues, friends, and family know about your "Do Not Disturb" policy. Consider using a visual cue, like a sign or closed door, to signify that you're in deep work mode.

If you find it hard to focus at home, change your environment—go to a library, a café, or a quiet space where you can work without disturbance.

The Day of Action

5. **Prioritize and Organize:**

   A successful MAD starts with a clear direction. Begin by writing down everything you aim to accomplish. This is your roadmap for the day, the outline of the masterpiece you're about to create.

   Once you have your tasks listed, prioritize them according to importance and urgency.

   By organizing them, you ensure that you're tackling the most critical tasks first. Without this structure, you risk drifting through the day, reacting rather than proactively pursuing your objectives.

6. **Take Regular Breaks to Recharge:**

   Your brain is like a muscle—it needs rest to perform at its best. Plan short breaks every 60 to 90 minutes.

   These pauses are essential for recharging and maintaining your focus. Use this time to stretch, take a walk, or grab a healthy snack—think fruit, not candy bars. Hydrate yourself, as well; keeping your body fueled ensures your mind stays sharp and your efforts remain sustained.

7. **Evaluate Your Progress and Adjust as Needed:**
   As your MAD draws to a close, take a few moments to reflect on the progress you've made. How much of your plan did you execute? What obstacles did you encounter, and how can you overcome them in the future? This is a critical step in continuous improvement. If you underestimated what you could achieve, aim higher next time; if you overestimated, adjust your expectations. This reflection ensures that each MAD becomes more effective than the last.

8. **Reward Yourself:**

   After a day of focused, intense action, take time to reward yourself. This is not just about enjoying a treat—it's about acknowledging your hard work and reinforcing the habit of taking massive action. Whether it's a walk in the park, a relaxing bath, or watching your favorite show, choose a reward that rejuvenates you. Celebrating your progress strengthens your resolve to keep going and creates positive associations with your efforts.

Moving Forward with Momentum

9. **Reflect on the MAD Experience:**

   Reflect on the results of your MAD and ask yourself: "Would another MAD be beneficial?" If so, schedule your next one. Building on the momentum of your previous MAD, you create a powerful cycle of focused effort that drives you closer to your vision. Success isn't built on isolated bursts of activity—it's the consistent, compounded effect of taking massive action over time.

10. **Commit to Future MADs:**

    The final step is making a commitment to yourself: pick a date for your next MAD. It's not just about scheduling; it's about a promise you make to yourself to keep moving forward. Every MAD is a chance to reset, refocus, and accelerate your journey toward your goals.

The Power of MAD

Massive Action Daily is more than just an occasional productivity hack; it's the key to unlocking the full potential of your dreams. By embracing MAD, you are not just hoping for success—you are taking deliberate, focused action to make it inevitable.

Remember, success is a journey, not a destination. But each step you take, each MAD you schedule, propels you closer to where you want to be.

"The future belongs to those who believe in the beauty of their dreams." — Eleanor Roosevelt.

Now, go ahead. Take that first step. The time for action is now.

CHAPTER SUMMARIES

Chapter 1: Storytelling and Story Analysis

In this chapter, you learned the importance of storytelling and how to analyze your story. Your personal story is the foundation for your messaging, and understanding its impact can help you connect with your audience on a deep level. By refining your story, you create a strong narrative that resonates with others and serves as a powerful tool in your business or personal growth.

Chapter 2: Crafting Your Vision

This chapter emphasized the significance of having a clear vision. You were encouraged to identify your long-term goals and create a picture of the future you want to achieve. Crafting a vision is essential for guiding your decisions and staying focused on what truly matters.

Chapter 3: Reverse Engineering Your Vision

To make your vision a reality, this chapter helped you break it down into smaller, actionable steps. By reverse-engineering your vision, you can see the steps you need to take, creating a clear roadmap that moves you from where you are now to where you want to be.

Chapter 4: Turn Your Vision into a To-Do-List

Once you've broken down your vision, this chapter guided you on how to turn your vision into a practical to-do list. Breaking your goals into specific tasks makes them more manageable and achievable. This ensures that you stay on track and focused on what needs to be done to move forward.

Chapter 5: Program Your Brain and Subconscious Mind

The power of your mind is limitless, and this chapter focused on how to program your brain and subconscious to align with your goals.

By using techniques like affirmations and visualization, you can rewire your mindset to support your success and build new neural pathways that foster positive habits.

Chapter 6: How to Hypnotize Yourself for Greatness

Here, you learned how self-hypnosis can help you unlock your full potential. Through deep relaxation and focused concentration, you can create new thought patterns that encourage success, remove mental blocks, and boost your confidence to reach your goals.

Chapter 7: Restate Your Intentions

Reaffirming your intentions is critical to maintaining focus and clarity. This chapter encouraged you to frequently restate your goals, keeping them fresh in your mind. By doing so, you reinforce your commitment and enhance your motivation to stay on track.

Chapter 8: How to Manifest Wealth and Success

Manifesting success is not just about wishful thinking. This chapter shared techniques to align your actions with your intentions. By staying focused on your goals and taking consistent steps, you can attract the wealth and success you desire.

Chapter 9: How to Sell Yourself to Others

This chapter covered the importance of selling yourself effectively. Whether you're pitching an idea, a product, or yourself, knowing how to communicate your value to others is crucial. Mastering this skill allows you to build relationships, gain trust, and create growth opportunities.

Chapter 10: Build and Develop a Team

Success is rarely achieved alone. This chapter taught you how to build a strong, supportive team.

It covered strategies for attracting the right people, fostering collaboration, and ensuring everyone is aligned with the vision and goals.

Chapter 11: Create Your Marketing Strategy

In this chapter, you were introduced to the concept of creating a tailored marketing strategy. By understanding your target audience, identifying the right channels, and crafting a compelling message, you can reach more people and grow your brand or business.

Chapter 12: Get MAD (Massive Action Daily)

Chapter 12 is all about taking **Massive Action Daily (MAD)**—dedicating yourself to taking bold, focused action toward your goals. It's about fully committing to progress and pushing yourself past obstacles. MAD days allow you to make significant strides in a single day, concentrating on one goal at a time and making it a priority.

To prepare for a MAD, you should:

1. Focus on one goal at a time, creating major progress by concentrating all your efforts on a single objective.
2. Schedule it in advance as a priority appointment.
3. Prepare your tools and materials before the day starts, so you can hit the ground running.
4. Minimize interruptions by letting others know about your focused work time, and consider relocating if needed for optimal concentration.
5. Prioritize and organize your tasks to make sure you're tackling the most important ones first.

6. Take breaks to maintain energy levels and avoid burnout.

7. Reflect and reward yourself after a productive MAD and adjust your strategies for future action days.

By taking **massive action daily**, you gain momentum that propels you closer to your vision. MAD is a tool for breaking through barriers, making significant progress, and transforming your dreams into reality.

Conclusion

The journey from **storytelling to taking massive action** is an ongoing process. Each chapter has helped you take concrete steps toward achieving your vision, programming your mindset, building meaningful relationships, and pushing past your limitations. The final piece of the puzzle is **taking massive action daily**. By committing to MAD, you set yourself up for success, focusing all your energy and resources on one goal at a time and ensuring consistent progress.

Now, it's time to take massive action. Don't wait for the perfect moment—create it. Start today and keep moving forward every day with relentless focus. Massive action is the key that unlocks your true potential, propelling you to greatness.

COACHING OPPORTUNITY

As much as I've poured my heart, experience, and strategies into the pages of this book, there's only so much that can be conveyed in writing. Transformation isn't just about knowing what to do, it's about having the support, guidance, and accountability to actually do it.

For some of you, this book will be the spark that ignites incredible change. But for others, the journey ahead may feel overwhelming. You might need someone to help you unpack your story, reframe your mindset, and guide you through each step of building the life you've dreamed of.

That's where coaching comes in. Imagine having someone in your corner, walking with you through the process, keeping you focused, and holding you accountable as you break through barriers and take intentional action. Together, we can go deeper, tackling the unique challenges and opportunities in your life to create a customized roadmap for success.

If you're ready to take this work to the next level, I invite you to book a call with me. Let's talk about where you are, where you want to go, and how I can help you get there. The hardest part is taking the first step—but once you do, everything can change.

Your future is waiting. Let's sculpt it together.

Book Your Call Today!

https://calendly.com/masterspeakersacademy/30min

https://www.gerardgrogans.com